Tumbleweed

A Story of Struggle

By Josefine Tilton

An autobiography

Edited by Frank Tilton
Copyright 2016

Tilton, Josefine. 1945-
Tumbleweed, A Story of Struggle
/ Josefine Tilton.

Includes author bibliographical data.

ISBN-13: 978-1539849933

ISBN-10: 1539849937

BISAC: Biography / Immigrant

1. Women —Immigration, Cancer survivor, Careers

MS18.P2016
416-ms37

First edition: Mar 22, 2012, Kindle Edition
Second edition: September 2016

Published in the United States by
https://www.createspace.com/6513742

1098765432-15

Contents

4

For Käthe and Herbert

I thank my parents who suffered and sacrificed so much in order for me to be free.

A Chair Collapses

Tumbleweeds typically spend more time snagged on fences than they do on the telephone. But this tumbleweed is one of the telephone company's best customers. It was a Saturday, the first week of a warm Indiana June when I called my mother in Germany. I was making my weekly call to check on her and my dad, better known to me as "Mutti" and "Vati."

It was 1993 and we were, and still are, able to "hug" each other only every few years. So the phone line was my only immediate connection to my parents. That particular Saturday call, however, was not at all "the usual." In fact, since that call, "the usual" has ceased to exist. I very nearly ceased to exist. Oh, I'm still a tumbleweed. I was a tumbleweed before calling Mutti, and I have been a tumbleweed since that call. There are still plenty of rusty barbed-wire fences out there for me to snag myself on. But, "the usual?" Not at all. That ended when my mother's chair collapsed.

My mother had fallen victim to her office chair a few weeks prior to that Saturday phone call. The chair had collapsed as she sat on it. She broke her ankle. A really serious fracture. There had been surgery and metal pins. She needed to sit with her leg elevated for several weeks to allow it to heal. This meant that she no longer could care for my father who suffered from Parkinson's disease. Caring for someone with

Parkinson's is itself a tough assignment. But my father had also lost a leg to a land mine in World War II. So my mother faced additional challenges when Parkinson's revealed itself. At the time of this phone call, she was 68, and, thanks to that faulty office chair, she could neither stand nor walk. I felt the agony in her voice. Never before had my mother been unable to care for my father.

"The boys have been good about helping," she told me. She meant my three brothers.

"And I've been okay with arrangements for someone to come in and help out. But the boys have their own families and their careers. Everybody is so busy these days."

She went on to tell me she was unable to find anybody to help out for the next two weeks. She cried on the phone. I had never heard or seen my mother cry. She was a strong woman. Still is. Always in control of her emotions, at least in front of us kids.

"Wieso niemand?" I asked. How could it be that no-one can help?

She unloaded the details. It simply amounted to the fact that all three of my brothers and their wives had exhausted their options. It wasn't a lack of willingness.

My mother didn't ask me for help, and didn't expect any. She knew that I lived in America. She knew that I, too, was working. And she knew the distance. She and my father had made the 4, 300-mile flight in years past.

"I'll call my brothers," I told my mother. "Maybe we'll come up with something." She agreed, but didn't sound convinced.

What I did instead was discuss the phone conversation with my husband, Wes (Wes was his middle name and still today my parents and brothers call him that). He was a teacher and was home for the summer vacation. He had a trip planned to California in three weeks to meet with our son, Eric. They had planned to go camping in the Sierra Mountains.

"Pack my suitcase. I'll go and take care of your parents for the next couple of weeks," he said. "You know that your parents are also my parents. I can drive to Dover Air Force Base. From there I can get a hop to Germany," Wes said without hesitation.

He was also a retired Air Force officer and, therefore, was able to catch overseas hops on military flights. I gathered his clothing and packed a small suitcase. Within two hours he was on his way to the East coast, about a 16-hour drive from Indiana.

I didn't call my mother back since Wes and I had decided his visit was to be a surprise. One of my brothers, Joerg, would still be with her for a couple of days. That gave Wes time to travel. He called me from Dover in the morning to let me know that he had arrived. He said there may be a flight out to Frankfurt via Lakenheath Air Base, in England, that morning, and the next time I would hear from him would be from my parents' house near Braunschweig in Northern Germany.

And thus began the end of "the usual." For starters, "usual" would have been both of us travelling to my parents. In our 30 years of marriage our trips back home to Germany had always been "we." But this trip wasn't "the usual."

We had become empty nesters. The kids had launched themselves out of the nest a few years earlier. Wes and I adjusted pretty well not having to fuss over the children. Our conversations now were about Wes' students in school and about my work in the Commerce Department. Of course, we missed our son and daughter, but we knew that we had to let them go to live their own lives.

Our son had found his new employment in California after graduating as an electrical engineer from Rose Hulman Institute of Technology. Our daughter, six months pregnant, had married her high school sweetheart after both graduated from college. They now lived in Germany. Her husband was an Air Force officer stationed near Ramstein Air Base.

I was still working for the U.S. Government, a career I started while Wes was stationed at Ramstein 1975-1981. Wes' final Air Force assignment brought us to Fort Benjamin

Harrison where he became an instructor at the Defense Information School. He retired at the end of that assignment after 23 years of service with the Air Force.

We remained in Indianapolis, and he followed his dreams and became a middle school teacher, teaching English and German. What an irony. When we met he didn't speak a word of German and I didn't speak much English, only what little I had learned in school in Germany. Now he was teaching my mother language after having gone to night school for 23 years earning two Bachelor's degrees and one Master's. German had been one of his degrees.

The day I first met Wes he had told me that he wanted to become a teacher after leaving the Air Force. His original plans were to serve four years and then go to college to get his teaching credentials. When I heard his words I thought, "Not another teacher." My Dad had been a teacher, which I hated all throughout my childhood. He never seemed to have any time for his own kids.

As for me, I have always loved challenges. I had overcome many challenges already in my life. Little did I know that the greatest challenge was yet to come. There would be no more of "the usual."

That Saturday afternoon after Wes began driving toward the East Coast trying to catch a hop to Frankfurt, I went to a nearby shopping mall to kill some time. Summer sales were already in full swing. I stopped in the lingerie department of a major department store and found a new bra. I really didn't need one, but because it was on sale I bought it anyway. It was a great bargain. I wore it to work the following Monday morning despite that it was hurting in my left breast. I thought perhaps I bought a size too small. When I came home from work I took it off and put it aside thinking I would exchange it the following weekend.

Wes arrived in Germany that Monday and surprised my parents tremendously. They had absolutely no clue that he would be the one who would take care of them for the following two weeks. Sure, they had three sons of their own, but they loved Wes as if he was another. They were happy and relieved. Their "Ami" son had come 4,000 miles to lend a hand.

"And the whole trip cost only ten bucks," Wes told me when he called from my parents' house. "I caught a contract civilian flight out of Philadelphia. It was dead-heading to Rhein Main Air Base to pick up dependent families headed back stateside."

"So, why the ten bucks," I asked. "I thought military flights were free."

"These days," he told me "they charge the ten bucks for in-flight meals. The flight itself was free."

"So, what did you eat for ten bucks?" I was curious.

"Nothing," he said. "I slept all the way across the Atlantic. I was so tired from the long drive to Dover, and there were only 20 passengers aboard. So I had a whole row of seats to myself. I put the seat arms up, stretched out, and slept."

"Did you stop to see Iris at Ramstein?" I thought he might have had a chance to visit our daughter before heading north to my parents.

"Didn't go that far south. We landed at Rhein Main, so I caught a bus around the runway to the Frankfurt civilian airport, went down to the train level, and headed north."

He told me he'd see our daughter on the return trip. And I didn't mention the painful bra I'd bought. That, too, could wait.

Wes took care of the daily cooking and cleaning and spent many hours discussing current issues--from politics to religion--which the Germans loved to do at each mealtime, and, of course, at afternoon coffee time. He learned how to bathe and dress my father. He ran errands, did the shopping, the laundry, even trimmed up my mother's garden. She was on the mend.

The following weekend I went back to the Department Store to exchange the bra. I bought a size larger and wore it to work the following Monday. The same thing happened. It hurt at the same spot. At bedtime I started poking and found a very large hard knot embedded deep in my left breast. This almost made me faint. This couldn't be, I thought? Hadn't I had a physical in January and a mammogram the year before? Besides I also examined my breasts on a regular basis. Everything seemed to be fine. It must be a cyst I thought. I called Wes the morning after that second shopping trip to let him know what I had found. I didn't want him to be worried. I wanted him to finish his two weeks at my parents' and come home on the arranged date.

In an effort to get my mind off the breast condition, or more likely because I had begun to fear where this could lead, I started to think back to my heritage and all the struggles I had gone through during my life as a tumbleweed. It was an easy segue into my past because my daughter Iris was now living in Germany's Rheinland Pfalz, not too far from where I had spent the final years of my childhood and where I had met Wes. So it was easy for me to visualize her and her whereabouts. She was expecting her first child. They had been married for seven years. She had had two previous miscarriages and was so happy to find out that she was pregnant again. I told her "It must be the water." I was especially happy that my grandchild would be born in Germany, not too far from where Iris herself was born, and where I had lived for nearly 11 years.

Where I came from

First, just a wee bit of a geography lesson may help you visualize where I, the tumbleweed, first took root.   Most Americans who travel to Germany are familiar with the fairytale castles and the Alps, those snow-capped ski resorts in Bavaria. That's the south of Germany.

Few Americans, however, are familiar with the German state of Saxony, my homeland. That's because at the time I was born just after World War II, Saxony, including my village of Kleinforst, on a hillside just outside of Oschatz, was "behind the Iron Curtain."

Cross Saxony's eastern border and you're in Poland. Cross the border to the south, and you'll enter the Czech Republic (formerly Czechoslovakia). Berlin, today once again Germany's capital city, is well to the north of Oschatz.   I, the tumbleweed, came to be born into the war-weary state of Saxony just after it was occupied by angry Russian soldiers.

My story begins in April 1945 though I wouldn't be born until December of that year. My father, Herbert, was a neighbor and a friend of my mother's brothers. He was at home on convalescent leave for two weeks to see an orthopedic doctor. He had been a soldier in the German Army from January 1941 to April 1945.

Both of my parents were called into service during the war, as were thousands of other Germans. They did what they had to do to stay alive. Military service did not make Nazis of them. While assigned to the Russian front where he was installing and repairing communications lines, my father lost his lower right leg during a land mine explosion near Smolensk, Russia. After the injury they moved him to the Ministry of Aviation located in Berlin and later transferred him to Dessau.

Dessau was not a particularly good place to be at that point of the war. Though away from Berlin, which was about to be demolished, Dessau was just a few miles from Torgau on the Elbe River. This is where, just a few days after my father's arrival in Dessau, American forces were about to meet with advancing Russian troops as the two nations put the final crush on German forces. And there was my father – well, okay, he wasn't yet my father, but he was soon enough to be – with one leg missing.

He didn't stay long at Dessau. Things were about to go from bad to worse for him. When Göbbels announced "total war" my father was ordered back to the front. In desperation, the German leadership was sending a freshly injured one-legged man 120 miles east to help stop the Russian advance at Hoyerswerda, near the Polish border. But, before he was to report to his new assignment, my father was allowed to spend a couple of days in convalescence at his home in Kleinforst on the outskirts of Oschatz. There he spent most of the time at my mother's house.

His step-mother had little understanding of or interest in the military, much less in him. But, his assignment to Hoyerswerda was short lived. He never told me why, but shortly after his arrival at "the front" he was again "reassigned." It is likely he arrived at Hoyerswerda from the west at about the same time as the Russians arrived there from the east.

His new assignment was to Außig. This was west of Hoyerswerda and just a few miles north of his home near Oschatz. But to reach Außig he would have to cross the Elbe River as he had done on his way to Hoyerswerda. On April 22nd he left by bicycle for Außig with his replacement prostheses strapped tightly on the back of his bike. It wasn't an easy task with one leg, but he managed to get around. So, there he was, on his bicycle, approaching one of the last remaining bridges spanning the Elbe River. Fate must have brought him to this place. The guard on the Elbe River Bridge in Meißen noticed his prostheses and his paperwork stating that he was from Oschatz.

"You have only one leg. How can they send you back to the war?" a compassionate guard asked quietly.

Stricken with fear, Herbert didn't know how to answer. Most guards weren't interested in anybody's situation. Why was he? What were his motives?

"I've heard rumors that the war will be over soon," the guard confided. "So go home before the guard on the other side of the bridge sees you," he continued.

Herbert didn't think he had understood correctly. "He wants me to go home? I have orders. They'll shoot me if they find out that I am a deserter," he said to himself. He was shaking but didn't waste a minute to take his advice. He reached into his bag and gave the guard a bottle of Schnapps that he carried on the back of his bicycle. He thanked the guard and disappeared before the other guard was able to notice him.

"I have been discharged as a war invalid," he told the authorities after he arrived back in Oschatz. Looking at his amputated leg, they accepted his "discharge" without any further questions. They provided him food stamps and told him to go home. Instead of going to his own house he went to my "soon-to-be" mother's house where my grandmother and my mother advised him it might be safer for him to visit his aunt in the nearby village of Schmorkau for a while. They thought he'd be safer there since no one who knew him would see him there. After all, the war was still going on, and one had to be wary of Nazi informers.

"Solche Schweine gibt es immer noch," my mother said referring to "pigs" who would inform on their own neighbors.

Just five days later, Oschatz was handed over to the Americans. People started to celebrate and display white flags as a symbol of surrender. The next day some people looted the German Army's food storage facilities and the local manor's potato distillery. The dire consequences of war were starting to show. The villagers had long had scarcely enough food for nourishment and took any opportunity to quell their hunger.

In desperation, and to numb their fear, my grandparents told me, "We were so terrified we tried to calm ourselves by adding potent spirits we distilled ourselves to peppermint tea." They had brewed tea from plants they had grown in their garden. Their anxiety over what would happen next was too great.

They were right to be anxious.

The Russians

On May 5, 1945, the peaceful hand over to the Americans ended. Russian tanks rolled into Oschatz. The racket could be heard at my grandparents' house which was about a mile away. Their fear turned into utter helplessness. A small delegation of Americans was still in town meeting with authorities. These Americans greeted the Russians and then left. The Russians took the city.

One month later around 2 p.m., 20 Russian tanks rolled into my parents' neighborhood. The soldiers parked the tanks and seized several homes. One house was used for their mess hall, and officers took other houses to use for their lodging. The German families of Kleinforst were forced to house, feed, and do laundry for the Russian soldiers.

My grandmother and her sister spoke Polish and could to a degree communicate with the soldiers who approached her house. She whined that everyone was sick in the house and had a contagious illness which was spreading around the neighborhood. This frightened the soldiers and they left. That first night was quiet but frightful for everyone.

It was a fearful time. Once in a while screaming of a woman or young girl could be heard while they were being raped. The Red Army set up a Command Post in Oschatz and seized all German military installations in Saxony just as they did throughout what was quickly becoming the "Soviet Zone of Occupation."

The Americans in the meantime moved back toward Torgau, north of Oschatz. It was there that the official "meeting" of the American and Russian forces took place.

But in Kleinforst, as with Oschatz itself, every night the neighborhood was terrified, afraid that the Russians would come looking for alcohol, threaten with their bayonets, and rape the women and young girls.

Fear and uncertainty gripped our entire village. My mother told me how she felt at the time.

"The authorities announced all locals must turn in any weapons they possessed," she said. "That heightened our anxiety because your grandfather and my brothers hadn't yet returned from the war."

Herbert was still in Schmorkau. They felt they needed his support now that the war was over and no one seemed to know what would happen next. So Mutti decided to pick him up. On their return trip home she secured on her bicycle carrier a small pistol wrapped in a white handkerchief. The pistol had been given to Herbert by a German soldier who wanted to fight his way through to get home. Instead of giving it to the authorities, the soldier gave it to my father who decided to keep it.

Back at my grandparents' Herbert suggested that all the women and young girls should hide in his parents' hay loft and that he would guard the area using the pistol. In short order there were about 20 villagers there every evening hiding.

One evening, however, my mother did not go into the barn. Perhaps it was fate. From her yard she had witnessed how her neighbor across the street had gotten raped by one of the Russian soldiers. Another neighbor had been digging under his berry bushes when he witnessed the same. That neighbor took my mother and his own daughter and hid them throughout the night.

The next morning Herbert rushed to my grandmother's and reported that some informer must have given the hiding place away. The Russians were at his house, discovered the hay loft, and had taken the first female they could find. He himself scrambled the best he could over a fence to get away to warn my grandmother that the Russians insisted they would keep looking until they found more women. Since my mother had not gone to the hay loft that night she was spared.

A day later my mother returned home from hiding when she experienced something terrible. The whole house smelled like gasoline and cologne. How it had gotten to be that way reveals much about the conditions in the village of my childhood. What she smelled was her own cologne. She had been saving it for special occasions. She had brought it back from France while she herself was posted there for her obligatory military service. The gasoline smell in the house, however, was a mystery.

A Russian soldier had come to my grandmother's the evening before. He was looking for a woman he could have sex with. My grandmother explained to the Russian in broken Polish that there were no other women besides her in the house. In response he got angry at being turned down and demanded with a pistol at her head, "You find me a woman right now, or I'll kill you."

"You must believe me, I don't have any other women in my house," she cried. Stricken with fear she remembered that there was a young woman in the village who neighbors reported had willingly slept with Russian soldiers.

"Ordinarily," Mutti told me, "such a woman would be scorned. But in these fearful times, the villagers seemed to think 'better that, than to have my own daughter raped.' So they sort of looked the other way."

"I will take you to a woman," my grandmother said, "but you have to take the pistol away from my head."
She led the soldier further into our village.

"This soldier is looking for a woman to have sex with. If he doesn't get what he wants, he will kill me and you," she told the woman at the door. "Please, you can save us and yourself," she pleaded with the woman.

"OK, I will follow you to your house. I do not want this guy in my own house," she replied and followed both of them to my grandmothers'. Mama, my grandmother, was relieved that she found someone for him, but the soldier, still not satisfied, demanded alcohol.

"I don't have any alcohol in my house," she explained. Again he held the pistol to her head and demanded she find some. She took him to an acquaintance knowing that he had recently picked up a few bottles of champagne some villagers had hidden in silos outside the city. The acquaintance denied having any in his house. Still with the pistol at her head Mama returned home. The woman who had agreed to have sex with the Russian soldier was still waiting in my grandmother's living room.

The Russian began to lose his patience and started to rampage throughout the rooms searching for alcohol. He seemed to forget that the woman was still sitting on the couch. During the search he found 20 eggs which Mama had hidden for Mutti's birthday cake.

"You can't have these eggs," she yelled trying to push him away. He, however, didn't care. He took the raw eggs and slurped them down one by one. He soon fell asleep on the couch with his pistol by his side. The woman was still sitting next to him. He hadn't touched her.

At 4:00 the next morning Mama heard clanking and shouting as the Russian tanks were getting ready to leave. She woke the soldier up and spoke in Polish that the Americans were coming. He jumped up, took my mother's large bottle of cologne, and poured it into a wash basin. He washed himself with it splashing it furiously over himself and all over the room. Afterwards he went to find his motorcycle which he had parked in the hallway inside the house. At this point he noticed that the small amount of gasoline he still had in his tank had leaked onto the floor. Shouting some mixture of Russian and Polish, he made it clear that my grandmother was to find him some gasoline immediately. In terror Mama took him to a neighbor who also had a motor bike. He saw the terror in her eyes and gave the soldier half a liter.

The soldier thanked Mama for the lovely night. As he left, he informed her that he would bring 30 of his comrades the next evening," Mutti sagged like a wet washcloth as she finished the story. "And the house smelled for weeks of gasoline and cologne."

Totally strained from the long night without any sleep Mama and my mother worried from hour to hour about whether or not the soldiers would come that evening. They didn't. Instead two different soldiers came to the neighborhood. These two had left their brigade and committed a series of robberies. They stormed into the homes and robbed the people of their watches and jewelry and totally destroyed everything.

Within a short time ten former German soldiers in civilian clothing gathered around. They had been AWOL (absent without leave) and were hiding in various homes in order to avoid imprisonment. They sneaked around the homes where the two Russians rampaged. Ripping the door open they shouted in Russian:

"тяните ваши руки, или мы стреляем - Put up your hands or we shoot!"

Totally surprised and shocked both Russians lost their guns. The Germans picked the weapons off the floor, held them up to the Russians' backs and pushed the two out the door and across the street and down a slope to the creek where the soldiers took off running.

The next morning two Russian officers arrived with an order that all Kleinforst men must meet in the stone quarry behind the settlement to be shot. They had heard that a "German resistance force" called "Wehrwölfe" had been in the village confronting their two troops the day before. After long negotiations between the Russian officers and Herbert's father, who worked for the Army weapons depot and who also was a member of the German Communist Party (KDP), the order to shoot the men was cancelled. It was into this fear-infested and uncertain environment a tumbleweed was about to sprout.

Herbert was with my mother every day. He felt he was responsible for her and was therefore protective of her. He didn't want her to be a victim of the Russians. There was a lot of hunger and poverty. The Russian military needed all the additional food that was available, and that didn't leave much for the local people. My mother later told me, "We were given food stamps and stood many hours in line for basics like a pound of sugar."

Life started slowly to normalize. My mother went back to work at a felt manufacturing company, and Herbert found a job at the county office. On her 20th birthday in June my mother learned that she was pregnant with me. She confronted Herbert and blamed him that he had ruined her life and that she never wanted to see him again.

Her reaction was solely a product of the stress born of the daily struggle for survival and the barbaric behavior of the Russians. Both Herbert and Kaethe, in a few short weeks to be my parents, had other partners in mind for a future that would never materialize for either. They had been neighbors and friends. They had been terrified and injured by war and its aftermath. And, yes, the "birds and the bees" function about the same in Germany as they do everywhere in the world. But Kaethe's heart was with a young man, Arthur, who did not return from the war. Arthur's last known assignment was aboard a submarine somewhere in the North Sea. And

Herbert? He was engaged to a girl in Berlin. That girl later died of blood poisoning while Berlin was a pile of rubble. More consequences of war. What chance would a fresh, gray-green tumbleweed have?

It was December 23, 1945, when Mutti, who was then seven months pregnant with me, together with her Uncle Hans, decided to go to Herbert's father to ask for some flour for baking Christmas cookies and bread. At that time Mutti still lived with her parents in Kleinforst. Our village was separated from the larger town of Oschatz by a beautiful park, about two miles of gently sloping, mostly wooded hillside leading toward Oschatz. About half way down this now snow-covered hill – for it was late in December – was another little village, Altoschatz. Both Altoschatz and Kleinforst were communities of farmers and blue collar workers. It was to Altoschatz that Uncle Hans and my mother were headed.

"Uncle Hans and I walked toward Altoschatz together," my mother told me, "partly to protect me from any Russians, but also to hold my hand. It was icy and snowy."

Uncle Hans was a big fellow with closely cropped white hair, alert eyes and large hands. He had served in both world wars, and was the sort of man not even a squad of Russians would risk tangling with. He was a good companion for my mother to have in this journey for a few handfuls of baking flour.

Herbert's father, Leo, from whom they hoped to obtain the flour, lived on a large manor in Altoschatz. This manor, somewhat similar to a Virginia gentleman's plantation in America, had been confiscated by the Communists. The property once belonged to a former landed aristocrat. But East Germany's post-war communists had wasted little time before grabbing the spoils, also known as "land redistribution." This manor had been divided among seven farmers and refugees from Schlesien who had been granted rights to cultivate these confiscated hectares. Leo managed these farmers and ensured that the crops were delivered to the appropriate authorities to feed the Russian soldiers.

"What do you want from me? We don't have enough to eat ourselves. We have to give everything we harvest to the Russians. Besides, I don't want to have anything do to with you and your unborn child," Leo shouted at my mother. "That child is not my son's. So go back home," Leo continued.

Empty handed, she and Uncle Hans turned and left. He wanted to pummel some sense into Leo's head, but he was wise enough to resist the temptation.

"Let's head back, Kaethe," he told my mother. "Leo will pay the price. When the time comes."

The wintery and icy conditions had made it difficult enough to walk down a small hill, especially for my mother who was seven months pregnant. And the return trip was equally treacherous.   Her uncle had promised my grandmother that he would hold on to her arm at all times to ensure that she would not fall.   But suddenly he sneezed and while he was cleaning his nose, Mutti slipped and tumbled down the hill.

"Ach, mein Gott!," uncle Hans screamed.   "Are you okay, Kaethe? I promised your mother I would take good care of you. And now this has happened? Let me help you up."

He held Mutti tightly under his arms, and slowly they walked back to Kleinforst.   Exhausted they arrived home without any flour.

"What happened? Why didn't he give you any flour? Mama (my grandmother) asked.

Mutti explained the heartless reception Leo had given them and told her that she had fallen on the ice.

"I especially sent Hans with you to ensure that you would be okay. I hope the baby isn't hurt," my grandmother said.

"That damned Communist! He only thinks of himself," Mama added. "I never did like him. He could have given you some flour. That certainly wasn't too much to ask for, especially since your child will be his grandchild," she shouted.

"He denied that his son Herbert is the father," Uncle Hans added.

"I am okay and the baby is fine. Just leave him alone," Mutti answered.

But the baby wasn't fine. The tumbleweed had been dislodged from its stem.

Two days later Mutti was in hard labor, and after she had coped 48 hours with unbearable pain, I was born, almost two months early. A midwife delivered me in Mama's house.

The first of my struggles had begun. My ear lobes, and fingernails weren't developed all the way. I weighed barely five pounds. The winter was harsh and cold. Not enough coal was available to heat the entire house, except the living room.

Mama, was desperate to keep me warm. She placed me in a small basket surrounded with warm bottles to keep me warm and alive. Goat milk kept me nourished. Mutti went back to work in an office during the day, while Mama took care of me.

Herbert stayed away. Among other issues, he was still committed to his engagement to the young lady in Berlin.

His career was about to change. Everyday life was regulated by the Soviet Military. As de-nazification was put into place the Communists were making decisions as to which teachers would remain in schools. Those who had been Nazi's would be fired. Several new teachers had to be hired even though some lacked any previous experience or higher education. In order to qualify for these positions, they had to complete a three-month crash course with additional ongoing studies to follow.

Herbert was one of those who was offered this opportunity. After three months he graduated and was assigned to the Elementary School in neighboring Altoschatz. Daily he rode his bicycle from Kleinforst to Altoschatz to teach. This was a distance of approximately one kilometers (half a mile). In the mornings he taught school, and in the afternoons he continued to study for his teacher's certification.

In March 1945, his fiancé in Berlin succumbed to blood poisoning. Shortly thereafter Mutti received notice from the Social Office that Herbert had accepted legal responsibility for being the father of her daughter.

Against her will, for she was yet uncertain about Arthur's fate, and after the begging of her father that she marry Herbert, Mutti began a dialogue with him. They wed in June 1946, six months after I was born. The sprouting tumbleweed's surname changed from Krell to Lohse. Kaethe and her tumbleweed moved in with Herbert's father, Leo, who was still living at the manor down by Altoschatz.

The tumbleweed's presence had a strange effect on quite a few names. Kaethe Krell, my mother, became Mutti. Herbert Lohse became Vati. And Mama, Kaethe's mother, who decided she wasn't yet old enough to be "Oma," insisted on being called "Mama." This was not a consequence of war. I have noticed that babies all over the world have a similar effect on family names.

Mutti spent most of the time at her own parents' to help them in their fields and to get food for herself and me. Food was extremely scarce. Arguments between her and Vati were an ongoing activity. Vati had no time for her and neither one was happy with the situation. She finally packed her bags and me and moved back into Mama's house.

"This is not the answer. You need to get back to your husband and work things out," Mama shouted and threw Mutti out of the house.

Since she had no other place to go she went back to Vati, and so they began the struggle to make their new lives work.

During 1948 we were still living in Vati's father's house. You'll remember Leo. The fellow who wouldn't give my mother a few cups of flour. In the meantime, he had moved from the Altoschatz manor back into his house in Kleinforst. The tumbleweed now lived upstairs in Leo's house just a few paces up the street from Mama's.

Leo had become Altoschatz/Kleinforst Mayor, a result of his Communist party membership. This position, however, was short lived due to his illness. Leo suddenly fell ill to life-threatening tuberculosis. The very contagious disease worsened, and we were ordered to move out immediately. The tumbleweed was "on the road again." This time we moved into an apartment in the Altoschatz school building where Vati was teaching.

Small German village schools commonly had classrooms on the bottom floor but also apartments above. These apartments were provided at community expense and offered to the teacher. In rare instances when a village school had more than one teacher, the "head" teacher would occupy the apartment. For my American readers, the term "Little Red School House" or "Little House on the Prairie" school will help illustrate the concept. Most often Germany's small village schools had but one teacher for multiple grades.

The former head teacher who had lived in the Altoschatz school apartment was one of those who had been fired during the denazification. The fact that Vati was the son of the Altoschatz mayor might also have played a role in us getting the apartment. Odd, though, that Herbert's father Leo was a Communist (hence "mayor") while my father Herbert was not. We'll see later what a huge role that played in the tumbleweed's odyssey.

So at this point the tumbleweed had sprouted on the Kleinforst hill, tumbled down that hill, blown back up the same hill, then bounced again down the hill to the Altoschatz school building. And all of this was but a harbinger of things to come.

We moved into the school apartment, but the place was totally without any furniture. It was as bare as the inside of an outhouse. So Vati traded in 10 pounds of glue he had saved from his earlier carpenter job and in this way came up with two beds. Mama gave us an old wardrobe cabinet, a table and a couple of chairs. The local Church offered a small piece of tillable ground for us to garden.

It was a daily struggle to get enough food on the table. Mutti stood in long lines at the store for whatever food might be available. Often, she came home empty-handed. Vati struggled in the classroom in the mornings, and in the afternoons he continued his studies. And all around us was the devastation of war. Sixty miles to our east lay the ashes of Dresden, firebombed by the Allies just three months before war's end. About the same distance westward the city of Leipzig was a pile of splintered rubble. Railways, highways, bridges, factories, power production. All in ruin. Hungry, shattered, unemployed survivors with weary eyes and pale faces filled the streets.

The tumbleweed didn't know it at the time, but she was fortunate to have sprouted in a small farming village. Fortunate. Despite tanks with red stars painted on them. Despite Russian soldiers – angry and often drunk – swaggering about. Despite over-eager, small-minded, newly minted Communist bureaucrats prying into every corner of daily life. Oh, yes, the tumbleweed was fortunate, indeed.

I was three years old when I was allowed to visit Mama on top of the hill in Kleinforst several times a week while Mutti was taking care of the latest addition to our family, my brother, Hans. The walk led me over a narrow-gauge steam train railroad crossing and a small bridge over a small stream. The street was graveled. The only car that occasionally passed was the post office truck. Others passing by were farmers sitting on wagons pulled by horses or oxen.

The farm house on the right side after the crossing intrigued me every time. I gathered goose feathers which I found and put them neatly into my little purse. These I carried to Mama. She and I made our own toys made of twigs, seeds and nuts and added the feathers as a decoration.

As I came around the bend where my mother could see me, she waved from the window letting me know that she was watching, and that everything was O.K.

My grandparents lived in a small two-story duplex on Paul Schuster Strasse, one of only four streets in Kleinforst. I loved it at Mama's. Her small kitchen was furnished with a wood-burning stove, one table and two chairs, one small kitchen cabinet and a sink. A large dark green tiled coal burning stove kept the adjacent living room cozy and warm. Her old grandfather clock in the corner chimed every fifteen minutes. A large dining room table stood in front of a camel-back sofa. Under the living room window Papa would place several large glass bottles. He used these to ferment fruit wine.

Down the hall towards the entrance was my grandparents' master bedroom with a window overlooking the barn yard behind the house. Upstairs were two bedrooms and a small nook that we used for a sort of kitchenette. The only bathroom in the house was downstairs next to a small pantry. It consisted of a sink and a toilette. We pulled a chain to flush the toilet. The chain was connected to a water tank which hung on the wall way above the toilet. It was a very sophisticated toilet for those days. Most of the neighbors still had outhouses. Inside the bathroom there was no means of taking a bath or a shower. For that, once a week Mama would fill warm water into a large tin bathtub that was located in our laundry area in the basement.

My grandmother told me another story about the toilet one day which made me laugh until I needed stitches in my side.

"A Russian soldier had come to our house for food," she recalled. "He took freshly picked cherries I had given him from our cherry tree and filled his helmet with them. Then he mumbled something in Russian that I didn't understand."

Mama seemed to relish this story. She went on and said, "I thought he needed to go to the bathroom. So I pointed to the door, and in he went. Before I could stop him, he emptied his helmet full of cherries right into in the toilet bowl and pulled the chain. He thought he'd be able to wash the cherries that way. To his surprise the cherries disappeared."

Now Mama's face darkened as she recounted the story. "He became angry and stormed into the kitchen. He sputtered and shouted a lot emotional Russian I didn't understand, but it was clear he was accusing me of having stolen his helmet full of cherries. He had obviously never seen such a toilet bowl and had no idea where his cherries went. Some of those Russian soldiers were ignorant rustics from somewhere behind the Ural Mountains."

"Get outside," the Russian soldier yelled. "Get everybody outside!"

Then Mama reminded me what she had often told me before. "Those Russians hated and despised us Germans. Don't forget, we Germans had invaded Russia. We might have killed someone in his family."

What Mama didn't tell me, probably because at that time no one really knew for sure, was that "we Germans" had killed very close to 20-million Russians in the war immediately before my birth. So, yes, she was right to fear that German soldiers might have killed members of this Russian's family. And that explains why her face hardened and darkened as she concluded the story.

"That Russian took us all outside and lined us up. He was getting ready to gun us down. I pleaded with him in Polish. That was as close to Russian as I could speak. Somehow, he finally seemed to understand. We had not stolen his cherries! Eventually I took him back inside and showed him the kitchen sink and explained the real purpose for the toilet bowl. Once he saw we had no outhouse, he seemed to understand."

More consequences of war. The tumbleweed was beginning to grasp why all the adults around her were so often so worried looking.

German Communists

My maternal grandparents had some livestock and maintained five acres of land. My grandfather – he had no objection to being called "Papa" – had been an airplane mechanic during the war and worked at a military base near Oschatz. The unit was moved to a secret location in the Erzgebirge and Papa was ordered to follow. After World War II ended, the Russians closed the base as they continued occupying the eastern part of Germany. Papa was out of his job. He walked home from the closed base. This took him several days.

After he returned he was ordered to report to the Russian Infantry which had taken up residence at the former Oschatz airfield. He was to report with blankets and clothing. The orders were that he and others were to be taken to Siberia. They made it as far as the Elbe River, and there they underwent a medical examination. A Russian nurse discovered that Papa had contracted malaria while he was stationed in Africa during World I. He still had symptoms. But this turned out to be good news. He was discharged from what would have been a prison detail and sent home by foot.

When Papa returned to Kleinforst his friend at the manor in Altoschatz offered him a temporary job as a welder. After six months the Communists confiscated and expropriated the farm. That was how he had received five acres of land which he was ordered to cultivate. He was told specifically what he had to grow and how much he had to harvest and deliver to the Russians in order to feed their troops. They did make some concession that if he did not have enough potatoes he could add carrots to fill the quota. However, it didn't leave much, sometimes nothing for his own family. They provided him a wagon, one plow and one 28-year old ox that took him to his fields every day. This was a 10 kilometer, several hours daily journey.

So, the tumbleweed received nourishment while Papa was in the fields and while Mama was taking care of chickens, pigs, turkeys, geese, and a goat. She kept a cow in the barn, too, and milked her twice a day. Her front yard was filled with fruit trees, and gooseberry and red and black current bushes. The fruit she canned, and the berries she turned into jelly, or used for wine. During my toddler and early school years Mama secretly filled her pantry and cellar shelves with jars hidden from the eyes of prying Communist block captains and roving Russian soldiers. She was determined to feed her tumbleweed and the rest of the family.

Every year Mama harvested her own seeds from vegetables. With these she was able to harvest fruit and vegetables from her gardens behind her barn and from a patch in front of her house, in an area most Americans would call a "front lawn." Secretly Papa would slaughter his pig during the night so the authorities and neighbors would not be alerted by his actions. The laws forbid to slaughter a pig without sharing with the neighbors.

"I do share, but with my large family," Mama would always say.

Mama had scrubbed her washroom in the basement days prior in order to prepare for the cooking and sausage making. She cooked the meat in the large round wash basin which was heated on the bottom. The sausages and bacon were smoked in her attic where she hid a small smoker. With all of this and with daily hard work, Mama was able to feed her family even through the difficult post-war years.

I should point out something here lest readers "over-visualize" what I've been trying here to describe. Perhaps you've had the experience of returning many years later to a house, a neighborhood, or a school of your youth. What seemed so very large to you as a child suddenly looks so pathetically small through the eyes of an adult. I had this very experience after the Iron Curtain ceased to divide Germany. When I returned to the small village of Kleinforst in Oschatz, my adult eyes saw Mama's house quite differently from the recollections of the toddler tumbleweed. Her house was a two-storey duplex with a total of maybe 900 square feet. Had the front yard been a lawn, it would have been possible to mow it with a hand-push mower in no more than 10-minutes. The "barn" was actually no bigger than a one-car garage with a loft. The rear yard, that source of so much fruit and vegetables, was actually larger than the house and the barn combined. In total, it was about the size of two American basketball courts without bleacher seating.

I enjoyed going out with Mama to glean the fields. After the farmers had been harvesting they'd give us the green light. We were allowed to pick up the remnants before the birds got it. The grain we found we'd use to feed Mama's chickens. Sometimes Papa flailed grain we gathered. This he then traded for flower at the local miller. We gleaned for potatoes and sugar beets each during their seasons. The potatoes went to feed to the pigs. The sugar beets we'd cook and press. The juice from these pressed beets Mama would slowly cook to a thick syrup. This we used instead of maple syrup.

While out in nature Mama taught me about different plants and trees, which plants were safe to eat or to dry for tea, and which were poison. Spending my childhood days with Mama was an education unto itself, but most importantly those early years with Mama shielded me. For the most part I was unaware of the extreme hardship around me.

As I grew older, Mutti would tell me, "Even the   daily necessities were a luxury. Nearly all food was rationed or not even available in stores," she said. "Without Mama's garden, we'd have starved."

Mutti and Mama stood many times in long lines in front of the grocery store. Sometimes they'd go at 3 a.m. just for a pound of sugar. Those who had food were ordered to share with others. Mama shared, but mostly with her own large family. Sometimes she'd barter with people who came from the cities and brought their silverware hoping to buy a few potatoes. Bartering, trading, and, yes, "forced" sharing, was very much a part of the tumbleweed's life in those post-war years.

One day after we returned from gleaning I had never seen Mama so angry. As we arrived at her house, the police were in the process of moving furniture out from my uncle's bedroom. Her son was away in Eberswalde studying to become a forester.

"We've been informed you have a room available," the policeman grunted. "This room must be given to a tenant. You know that no one is allowed to have unused rooms in their house," the policeman shouted.

My family never knew for certain which of the neighbors had "informed" the authorities. They did know, as did virtually all post-war Germans, that housing was scarce. Most of the large cities were heaps of rubble. Extreme measures were necessary to house the homeless. Few would argue that point, as a temporary solution. The newly empowered Communist bureaucrats of the "Soviet Zone," however, saw an opportunity to advance the cause of Socialism. The "temporary solution" became a means of inflicting punishment upon neighbors who "had more than the rest." Never mind the fact that hard work and sacrifice was what had resulted in some having "more than the rest."

"Besides," Mutti explained years later, "the housing shortage was in the cities.

"This is my son's room," replied Mama. "You cannot take this away from us. He is away in school and will come home on vacation. You have no right to force us to take strange people into our house."

The shouting went back and forth for a while until the police left, leaving the bedroom furniture in front of her house. Mama and Papa moved the furniture back into the room but only for a short period of time. The government eventually won. She had to take a tenant, a man named Herr Schulze.

In 1949 the German Democratic Republic came into being. Industry was nationalized, and agriculture was collectivized. A state-controlled economy was created. People like my grandmother were forced to share their homes with strangers, and Rittergueter (manor) owners were dispossessed of their property by the Communists. These once aristocratic land owners were allowed to take only the clothes they wore when they were evicted. They went from owners of hundreds of hectares, and employers of servants and field hands, to common laborers. My aunt's father who owned a manor was shot and killed in front of her.

Vati once explained it to me this way, "The German Democratic Republic! Only one of those words is true. After the war we became a client state to the Soviet Union. That's not democratic. And we're certainly not a republic. So that leaves German. Well, that we are, in name at least."

As tumbleweed was growing, she began to notice that Papa was not a young man anymore. He had reached 60 years, and the tolls of two wars and years of hardship were beginning to slow him down. After three years working in the fields, he was no longer able to grow and harvest on his assigned plot. His ox had died and so he gave the five acres to someone else to manage. This angered the local Communists for he had not cleared the action with them. As punishment they placed him a night job as a boiler man in a dairy. It was one more intrusion of Communism into our daily lives.

For a while my parents seemed very happy in Altoschatz. The camaraderie among teachers was great, not only at work but socially as well. But then a Fasching party in February 1950 (Mardi Gras) changed everything.

"A fellow teacher invited us to the Fasching party," Mutti told me. "It was to be a costume party with the theme 'Graefin (countess) Marizza.' And in those desperate times, we truly needed a good party."

Mutti had hardly needed to tell me that. Even young and tender tumbleweeds can sense when all about them is crispy and tense.

"We all borrowed costumes from Frau Schubert, you know, the lady who was still allowed to live at the Rittergut after the estate had been taken from her."

Mutti told me that some of those costumes dated back to 1870. They had belonged to Frau Schubert when her husband was still alive and running the estate. She had always enjoyed dressing up at these Fasching parties and had kept those clothes as a reminder.

"The night of the party, your Vati and I were dressed up as a professor couple," Mutti said. "Not too original maybe, but, hey, the costumes were free."

The party lasted until the early morning hours. On their way home the group passed by farmers and blue collar workers who were on their way to work. Since the Communist-imposed curfew was midnight, these workers were surprised to see the teachers at early morning hours.

"They reported us immediately to the town Communist Party officials," Mutti's disgust spoke louder than her words. Such behavior, just as it had been under Nazi rule, was common practice among citizens. Not only was it mandatory to report people who were seen not "obeying" the law, but those making such reports gained favor with the Party authorities. That's how the system worked.

As a result of this "neighbor spying upon neighbor" report, the local Communist Party officials dismantled the group of teachers. At the end of the school year, reassignments scattered the group whose only crime against socialism had been having a bit of Fasching fun.

"Two of these teachers managed to escape to West Germany," I heard Vati tell Mutti. "I got off light," he said, "once again on the weight of my father's influence."

"Leo's an influence peddler," Mutti's voice was firm but her eyes were red and swollen, so I sensed an ill wind was about to whistle about my little tumbleweed arms.

"He's got them all convinced. Oh, how poor Leo suffered as a loyal communist when those Fascist Nazis were in power."

"Well, I managed to survive the Hitler years without becoming a Nazi," Vati spoke tersely but quietly, "and those damned communists won't get any more of my loyalty than the Nazis did."

I had no idea why Vati seemed to detest Communists and Nazis. But I was certain of one thing. When my parents whispered, it was a good time to listen. That was how I had found out about the stork. I had heard Mutti whispering that a stork was soon going to bring my second brother, Kerndl.

The "ill wind" did whistle. The tumbleweed soon landed in another nearby village. I was not yet a five-year-old when we moved to Luppa in the summer of 1950. That's what Vati had meant by "getting off light."

Luppa was a 600-year-old village that had two parts. The blue collar part of town consisted of row houses located along the main state highway which connected Leipzig and Dresden. The other part of town belonged to shop owners and supervisors of the large-acreage farmers, those who had overseen the manors before the Russians came.

At first Vati rode the train to Dahlen, a village near Luppa, and then walked the rest of the way to Luppa to teach. We stayed at Mama's until our apartment in the school was available.

The distance between Kleinforst and Luppa was 9 kilometers, about 5 miles. That may seem a short distance, but for the tumbleweed, living in Luppa meant I could no longer walk to spend my days with Mama. I wasn't so sure that Vati's "getting off light" meant that I was "getting off light." Still, we settled into our new location and lives, and I waited for the stork's delivery.

We spent Christmas that year with Mama and Papa in Kleinforst. And somehow that stork knew where to find us. Kerndl, my baby brother, was born on December 27th, the same day as my birthday only five years later.

We always enjoyed the holidays with a big family with three of my uncles and aunts and our cousins. We kids received no presents since nothing was available to buy. We didn't miss having presents either. We made our own toys from walnut shells, buttons, thread spools and other things. For us children, it was enough to have our family's love and the plentiful, if hoarded and garden grown, food in Mama's house. During the Christmas holidays Mama baked several Christmas Stollen, a German fruit cake. She took her finished dough on large baking sheets to the local bakery for baking.

Mama had to be about as creative with her baking as we kids were with our handmade toys. If the recipe called for almonds, and we had none, she'd use pumpkin pits. These she'd saved from her pumpkin patch. When blanched, they could stand in for almonds. Occasionally, Mama received ingredients such as raisins and candied fruit from her brother in West Germany. She was not always lucky to have those cherished ingredients, however. Sometimes her packages would be confiscated by the government authorities. Receiving packages from the "West" was considered capitalistic and was not allowed. Every action, it seems, was under intense scrutiny by the government. And that was why my parents often whispered.

Vati's job in Luppa turned out to be very stressful, and this would play a major role in the tumbleweed's next storm-driven relocation. While he was working daily as both elementary school teacher and principal, he was studying in the evening. He still had to complete his final exam to gain his credentials. His new fellow teachers saw themselves as being superior, and made no secret of it.

Mutti told me, "Vati doesn't yet have the same credentials they have. While he was away in the war they went to the university. They look down on him. And they resent it that he is principal. They forgot that where he is in his career, he had to work twice as hard," she continued.

I may have been too young to grasp all of this, but I certainly got the picture when the silkworms arrived.

"His fellow teachers," Mutti huffed. "They set him up!"

I had no idea how teachers and silkworms could "set" my father "up." But soon enough it became clear.

Vati got "hooked" into a science project which involved raising silk worms.

"The other teachers knew what a time-consuming project it was," Mutti complained. But they made it sound like there was nothing to it. A simple science project, they said."

So in July, 1951, silk worm eggs arrived in an envelope right at the beginning of the summer break. The other teachers headed out for vacation. Since we lived in the school house and it had a large attic, the teachers handed the project over to my parents saying, "Just follow the instructions that come with the eggs."

Stuck with the project, Mutti got up early in the morning and rode her bicycle to pick mulberry leaves for feeding. There was a large hedge which had been planted during Hitler's time just outside the village. This, we learned, was the ideal food for the silkworms. As the worms grew, the feeding had to be done twice a day, and my brother Hase and I had to accompany Mutti. We pulled a small wagon to collect the leaves. At first it seemed like great fun. But even fun becomes drudgery when it "must" be done.

Vati built several large temporary shelves for the 1000+ worms which began to grow into fat, off-white silk worms very fast. The feeding and cleaning began to be a huge task. Who would have thought cleaning up after worms meant daily changing of dung-stained newspapers with which we lined Vati's shelves?

It wasn't long before Mutti began to feel the strain.

"Herbert, I can no longer continue with this. I am at the end of my rope. Up the stairs, down the stairs, out to the mulberry bushes! Twice a day. Out and back! I'm trying to feed these 1,000 worms, our three kids, and you, and we ourselves have scarcely anything to eat!"

Mutti wanted time to plant and grow our own garden. And we kids wanted more time to play.

"I'm going up to Kleinforst to see my parents," Mutti cried one day. "I don't care what happens to these worms. You need to stay and finish your final exam," she said to Vati and then we left.

She walked the 9 kilometers to Mama's house pulling us kids in a wagon behind her. Two days later, Vati joined us.

"What happened to the worms?" Mutti asked.

"I don't know and I don't care. I had to study for the exam," Vati replied.

"We can't leave the project. They'll punish us for this. We have to leave right away," Mutti said.

Guilt driven, we returned to Luppa to see if the worms were still alive. We found that the worms were no longer worms instead they had spun themselves into small peanut like cocoons. They lay on the floor or hung on the roof beams. Diligently we collected the cocoons, and Mutti placed them in large cartons and shipped them off for silk spinning. As a compensation for her work, she received 15 meters of light blue silk fabric from which she made a dress for me and two shirts for my brothers.

As for the science teachers? They received a two-page handwritten report. They never learned about the blue silk fabric.

In 1952, although fully certified for teaching, Vati still had much to learn such as local school policies and guidelines.

The political situation made this task harder. Communist ruling had become more dominant. This affected everything from how a farmer could sell his pig, to what Vati must teach in his school. Vati was an honest, dedicated man, but he refused to bend under the pressure. He refused to teach what he knew to be untrue and refused to use his classroom to mold young people into Marxist puppets. He also refused to join the Communist Party. This would soon spawn ominous consequences for the tumbleweed.

In order to make ends meet, Mutti applied for and received a home economics teaching position for the villages of Luppa, Calwitz and Malkwitz. She began to teach girls how to sew, embroider, crochet and knit. The job required her to travel by bicycle to these villages every day and teach two hours after regular school hours. Teaching material such as yarn and fabric was hard to get. The local farmers graciously shared some of their material reserves.

Shortly thereafter, Mutti was "voted" to become the head of the local democratic women's organization. Morally she couldn't turn down the position as a teacher. She had to accept. As her first task she organized a trip for the women to visit the newly established Stalinallee in East Berlin. The Stalinallee was a show place for the working class. Berlin communists had created a new type of street life with restaurants, offices and shops mixed with housing all along the street. The interest level was very high.

Mutti arranged for and filled two buses. Even Mama accompanied the group. At Shoenefeld which was the passport control point, the women were checked for their authorized paperwork to enter East Berlin. Traveling to East Berlin required special permission because it was possible at that time to slip through the checkpoints and reach West Berlin -- freedom.

Before the trip Mutti had assigned Anna, a woman activist, to speak to the officials since she had previously been in East Berlin on several official occasions. She knew her way around and assured the border police that this was a legitimate trip, and she vouched that all the women would return. Only then was the group allowed to proceed.

Friedrichstrasse, a major East Berlin city-train station, was the bus' intended final destination for the group. From there the women could easily reach the working-class "show place."

Before Anna could gather the group to visit the Stalinallee, most of the women had disappeared. They had switched trains and were on the way to Gesundbrunnen in West Berlin. Gesundbrunnen had opened a special market for East Germans where they could buy so many items that were not available in East Germany.

Mutti and Mama, too, had disappeared from the Friedrichstrasse station. They went to visit an old friend who often came to Mama's house to trade household items for food. The friend had a fur coat and a hat, a lipstick and a pair of glasses, as well as some clothing waiting for them.

After visiting the friend, Mutti and Mama took the S-Bahn to Gesundbrunnen to the market to find the wool and pepper they needed. Despite the side trips, all the women arrived punctually back at the bus for the return trip to their East German homes.

Some women wore new shoes and others had bags filled with things they bought or bartered at the market. At the Schoenefeld pass control point Anna and her friend talked about the Stalinallee and the milk bar "Budapest" taking the attention away from any suspicious wrong doing, such as shopping in West Berlin. The women who went only to the Stalinallee, on the other hand, noticed the new shoes worn by those who had shopped in the West.

"They reported us to the police," Mutti told my father. I knew it was serious because Mutti whispered. "Those damned Communist sympathizers. There we were at the control point, and they reported us!"

"What did you do?" Vati asked her. "What came of it?"

"Nothing," Mutti sputtered. "Nothing happened. The policeman was only interested in our passports."

But it turned out to be more than "nothing." The next morning Vati was visited by two arrogant-looking men. They were County Council members. They had come to investigate.

"We understand your wife organized a trip to East Berlin, whereby several women crossed the border to go shopping," the official interrogated my father. "Don't you know that shopping in the West is against the law? You and your wife of all people should know this! Don't you know that for doing so you must be punished?" he continued.

Mutti stood besides Vati, white as a sheet. This was what all the whispering had been about. She and Mama were among the women who crossed the border. They had all returned. Still, somehow there was a crime.

Instead of a jail term, the Party leaders ordered my mother to attend the next Sunday church services to spy for them and report what the minister said during the services. At that time the Church was still allowed but carefully watched.

"So what have you heard this morning in Church, Frau Lohse? Anything you can report us?" said the official who was already waiting for her outside the Church.

"I can't tell you anything," she replied. "I fell asleep during the service," she continued.

The official was furiously "steaming."

"Apparently you are not fit even for this position. Now I must report you to the Party and make a recommendation to terminate you as the women's organization leader," he shouted and disappeared.

"Herbert," I heard my mother loudly whispering again later that afternoon. "What now? What are they going to do to us?"

"Nothing. That pig-dog!" Vati whispered so loudly they must have heard it all the way to the next town. Actually he said, "That Schweinehund!" The German expression sounds so much more powerful than its English translation.

"That stupid Schweinehund. He probably will do nothing. He tried to trick you into doing his job at the Church. That means he hasn't been doing it himself. If he reports you, he'll implicate himself!"

This time "nothing" seemed to mean just that. At least for a while.

The tumbleweed – even though I didn't yet know I was a tumbleweed – continued hearing anxious whispering.

While I was busy trying to be a kid, Communist ruling became more and more dominant in our daily lives. The local Party seemed to affect everything. There was ever more of the harsh whispering I was to hear.

"They want me to make 'good little communists' out of my students," Vati grumbled one night. "It's not history or social studies they want me to teach."

I began to worry about that word, "nothing." How many of those "nothings" could there be until "something" happened.

"They know I'm not a Communist. They know I haven't officially joined the party," was one of Vati's loud whispers to Mutti.

"That's why they're watching you, Herbert," Mutti said. "And watching me, too. I feel like they are wolves. They're just waiting for the best time to pounce on us."

Soon after I had begun to dream about wolves watching us, Vati went to a community meeting. Mutti made light of it, but I thought he was visiting wolves.

"What did they discuss, this time?" Mutti asked in a hoarse whisper after Vati returned.

"They want to change our village street names," he said. "We are supposed to change to all the street names to something acceptable to the Communist Party."

Vati told Mutti he had spoken up and expressed his opinion why they should leave the names the way they were. He said the attendees gave him a standing ovation.

But he told Mutti, "The party saw it differently."

I waited to hear the word "nothing." I didn't hear it. I wish I had.

Angered "party" leaders gave my father an added responsibility. He was to begin inspecting village farmers every

Sunday morning to search for butter, milk, eggs, and the like, which the farmers were compelled to give to the government.

"They want more food for the soldiers. The Russians. So now, I am to spy on my own neighbors!" Vati forgot to whisper this time.

"And while I'm snooping about," he whispered between his teeth in response to Mutti cupping her ear and placing her hand over her mouth, "I'm somehow supposed to convince the village people they should willingly accept the new communist regime."

"Ach, solche Schweine." It was clear to me Mutti was whispering about people, not the farmers' livestock.

"I am not a communist and do not want to serve as a hatchet man for the party," Vati had said. Again I did not hear the word "nothing," and I was pretty sure I would not hear it that day.

Times got harder and harder for my parents. Three children, and we barely had enough food to eat. One rainy evening Vati left the house and went to a potato field to harvest some potatoes. Shaken from the fear of being caught by the field control, he came home after only harvesting a few. That lasted only a couple of days. Mutti made daily trips to the nearest woods to hunt for mushrooms. Meat was a luxury. We ate meat only on Sundays. If it was available.

Could We Escape?

The political pressure on my parents grew stronger and stronger. Secretly during walks in the open field where they were assured no one could overhear them, my parents began to discuss ways they might escape to West Germany. They settled on a plan, and decided to put it into place. The first step would be to move out of the school house. The tumbleweed was about to roll once again.

My parents had learned that a former teacher who lived in a small row house on the other side of Luppa was planning on moving away. To take advantage of this opportunity they immediately requested a move to his house giving as a reason that the school apartment was too small for a family with three children. One of the other Luppa teachers had just married and offered to move into the school apartment. This was a perfect swap. Such exchanges were allowed according to the Party. Since they couldn't find any wrong doing, party officials granted the request.

Suddenly, though still in Luppa, the tumbleweed found herself living in a house located directly on State Road 6. This narrow highway led to Dahlen, the next small village some 3 kilometers distant. Our living room windows were facing the street. Between the front of the house and the sidewalk was a small patch of dirt. This would later play an important role, but for me it was of little value. It was too close to the highway for us kids to play, and it had no fruit trees or vegetables like those at Mama's Kleinforst house. The backside of the house bordered a small farm. Even that was no improvement for us kids since it wasn't our farm. The house was large enough for all of us, but it didn't matter much. The move only lasted a while. For the tumbleweed it was like being snagged at the foot of a split-rail fence and waiting for the wind direction to change. And change it would.

On June 18, 1953, Russian tanks came roaring around the bend on State Road 6 and almost ran into our "new" house. I was very frightened by the Russian soldiers. I remembered how they used to stand guard for hours at the side of my grandmother's property in Kleinforst. Sometimes they jokingly pointed their guns at me. I also overheard the whispered stories my parents and grandparents had told about the Russians immediately after the war. The memories of what they had done to ordinary people were still fresh.

These tanks, now once again before our very door, brought instant fear to my parents. They thought another war was breaking out. Glued to the radio they learned that there was an uprising in other parts of East Germany. The uprising began on June 17th as a demonstration against unreasonable production quotas, but it soon spread from Berlin to more than 400 cities, towns and villages throughout East Germany. As it spread, it also took on a more expansive political character. Beyond calls for labor reform, demonstrators began to demand more fundamental changes such as free elections. Chants were heard calling for "Death to Communism" and even "Long live Eisenhower!" This demonstration didn't last very long. The people lost. And eventually the Russian tanks moved on.

Despite all those happenings in Berlin, my parents still contemplated on a way to leave. Fragments of the whispers sounded more and more desperate.

"We cannot stay here."

"We've got to leave."

"There's got to be a way for us."

In the summer of 1954, Mutti began on several mornings to notice that the dirt strip below our living room windows was covered with footprints. In order to get to the bottom of this, she raked the dirt the night before only to find the fresh footprints again the next morning.

"Herbert," her hoarse whispers said, "I fear that someone is spying and listening to our conversations and reporting them to the officials."

The proof came one evening when my parents suddenly opened the front door just before they went to bed. They caught sight of a limping person running away. They had been speculating as to who it might have been outside our window. They recognized the man; he was an old Communist Party member and now a spy for the Socialist Unity Party, the new governing party of the German Democratic Republic.

"So now we know," Vati said. And this time it wasn't a whisper.

At 2:00 a.m. now tormented with fear, my parents woke us up. They hurriedly dressed us and said we were about to go on a trip.

"But, Mutti!" both of my brothers began to whimper.

"No 'But Mutti' now," she bent low to their ears. "And make not a peep!"

Outside the house ready to leave Mutti started to cry.

"Herbert, I can't do this. I am so afraid of the refugee camp. What happens if we get caught? They'll put us in jail. What will happen to the children?"

She stood at the steps as if she were frozen.

"I can't do it", she cried.

So we went back into the house. I had no idea what just had happened. Sleepy, I went back to bed. Mutti and Vati were still discussing the situation in harsh whispers as I fell back to sleep.

Soon Mutti began to make daily bicycle trips to Kleinforst. She was taking important family documents to Mama's house. She knew it was only a matter of time until something would happen to her and to Vati. The Party officials would find a reason to put them in jail.

A window of opportunity seemed to appear. Vati applied for a teaching position in Strausberg, north of Berlin, but was turned down. He had not been aware that the East German Military Headquarters was located in Strausberg and that only "selected" people were accepted to live in that town. That option no sooner evaporated than another began to emerge.

My parents decided to move to Mama's and try to find a new job in the area. The move to Mama, however, would only be possible if there was a house exchange available.

It's true that housing was scarce. War damage had made thousands of houses and apartments uninhabitable. People were not allowed to move from one place to another without "an exchange." This played right into the hands of the local communists. They used this administrative function, like most others, to keep their fingers on the pulse of every human activity.

Luckily my parents found a party member in Leipzig who was scheduled to be transferred from Leipzig to Luppa. He was willing to move into our house on the road to Dahlen. Meanwhile, Herr Schulze at Mama's, the fellow Mama and Papa in Kleinforst had been forced to house in my uncle's "vacant" room, wanted to move to Leipzig. That, in turn, allowed us to move to Mama's. This was the three-way house exchange that my parents needed. The request was approved. The Party officials had no clue and were surprised at my parent's organization but couldn't stop the process because it fit the legal criteria the communists themselves had established.

The tumbleweed was back in Kleinforst with Mama. That was good. But less so was this: I would have to go back to school down the hill in Altoschatz. Changing schools was always traumatic. There was little standardization among schools, especially in the smaller towns and villages. It seemed I always had to start over, or wait until someone else in the class caught up with where I had been in another school.

But my troubles were sawdust. My father's were wooden planks. Vati had thought that once in Kleinforst he could find a new job. Unfortunately this was a fallacy. Again, the communists. He had to continue his teaching in Luppa. That's where "they" needed him. So he rode his bicycle in rain, snow or ice every day for six months to reach the Luppa school.

While we lived in Kleinforst Mama listened on a daily basis to RIAS Berlin (Radio in the American Sector, part of Voice of America). She was listening for any new developments that might be useful to my parents. The East German radio station that she was "allowed" to listen to aired only communist propaganda. They reported nothing about West Berlin or West Germany. But Mama's listening to radio from the west was fraught with risk. Anyone who was caught listening to RIAS Berlin was to be arrested. And, of course, prying neighbors who might want to gain "influence" from the communists would be quick to report if they overheard "western propaganda."

But Mama was experienced in such things. "I've lived through two wars," she'd say. "There's more than one way to hang a hook on a fishing rod."

In order not to be caught, she turned on the water in the kitchen sink to muffle the sound of the radio broadcast. She'd press her ears tightly to the speakers to hear. Often she would mutter whispered complaints about East Germany suppressing the signal with scratchy sounds of interference.

"I need to know what is happening in the West, and how many people fled again today into Berlin and West Germany," she would tell me.

I knew what the "West" was. I had traveled once with her to the "West" to visit her brother. For me as a child it was a country of milk and honey. Everybody had enough to eat and didn't have to stand in line for things. People could buy things that we couldn't get such as chocolate, cocoa and coffee. One brief trip, and my taste buds had taught me to relish life in the "West."

I was scarcely a ten-year-old, and should have been more interested in school books and dolls. But the whispered tension of my parents, and Mama's trained radio listening had given me some interesting if disjointed facts about east and west, as we Germans spoke of it.

Not long after those Russian tanks had rumbled through the Kleinforst of my infancy, Germany had actually become two countries. The border between these two Germanys had been sealed by barbed wire, mine-fields, watchtowers and machine gun "free-fire" zones. But the border between East and West Berlin had remained open, but controlled with checkpoints at border stations. This was because the city was legally still under joint Allied occupation. Berlin was, and still is, a city the size of Chicago. But it was occupied and governed by the victors of WWII. British, French, and Americans occupied "West Berlin." The east part of the city was under Russian occupation. So going to "East Berlin" meant staying within "Communist" control.

East Germans outside of Berlin, like my parents, had to have permission to travel into East Berlin or, and this was rarely approved, to West Germany. Only trusted communists ever gained such permits. Small towns and villages, like our Kleinforst, kept watch on "suspected" people and created lists of those thought to be likely to try an escape. Some people who were on this so called "list" and who were caught attempting to escape found themselves in hard labor, some as far away as Siberia. The standard sentence was 25 years.

Yet, at the time the tumbleweed was bouncing between Kleinforst, Altoschatz, and Luppa, -- about 125 kilometers south of Berlin -- some 5,000 people daily managed to cross the border into West Berlin to seek refuge. Before the concrete wall went up, these refugees often succeeded in blending with daily commuter traffic through the nine checkpoints. These commuters were people who lived in one part of the city but worked in another. Because the numbers were so great, especially at "rush" hours, most of the checkpoints only "spot-checked" the crowds. This is why Mama tried so hard to listen to the American radio broadcasts from Berlin. That was the only source of information about what was going on in Berlin.

I was becoming increasingly aware that the rope was becoming tighter and tighter around my parents' necks. Since war's end my parents had been living under watchful eyes of the Party. We all feared it was only a matter of time until Vati would be called an "enemy of the regime" and put in jail. With a father labeled as such we children would not have had any opportunity for good education or for jobs since these benefits were available only for the children of faithful party members. The urgency of the whispering and the strained expressions on Mama's face as she pressed her ear to the radio troubled the tumbleweed's dreams.

It was December of 1954. The fragments of whispers I could hear had become ominous. It felt like one of those slow-building August storms with huge, dark clouds. Some nebulous giant was creeping toward us.

"I must go to Berlin," I captured from part of Vati's muffled, taut whisper.

"But Herbert ... refugee camps," was all I could decipher from my mother's response.

The next day, Vati was gone. There was no whispering. In fact, no one was talking at all. Vati stayed away from his teaching job in Luppa for two days. He had traveled to Berlin to meet with some friends. He was trying to find out how and if it was still possible to escape to West Berlin. Escaping as a family seemed no longer an option. Vati thought since Mutti was so afraid of the refugee camp he might find a way to escape alone and eventually get us all out of East Germany.

He was back in Kleinforst before the sun came up on the third day of his absence. The whispers, now sharp-edged and fast-paced, had returned with him.

"I managed to visit Marienfelde," he told Mutti, with Mama and Papa leaning to catch each word. "It's a refugee camp in West Berlin."

"You made it to the West?"

"Yes, it is possible. But risky."

"And the camp, Herbert? Is it as bad as we thought?"

"We wouldn't be there long."

"We?"

"The camp officials told me that it was not a good move for me to come alone. Instead, they told me to go back and pick up my family."

"Why?" three whispers erupted at once.

"I'd never get all of you out. A few were lucky at first. But it didn't take long for the damned communists to figure it out!"

He told them about families in the east being held hostage to entice escapees to return. He said some were jailed and their houses and all possessions were snapped up by the communists.

"There was nothing for some of the men to come back to."

"Ach! Herbert!"

"That's why we must go at the same time. Not as a family. We'll have to look like parts of different families. They also told me the type of family documents we should bring along so we won't get stuck in the refugee camp so long."

We kids were shoo'ed outside to play. We were even allowed to make noise. They didn't fool me. I figured out that our noise would allow them to whisper more clearly.

During Vati's absence the Party had interrogated Mutti about Vati's whereabouts. She explained that she didn't know where he was. She thought he might have checked himself in at the Wermsdorfer hospital with a nervous breakdown. She convinced them she was terrified at not having heard from him for two days.

In Berlin Vati had learned that escaping as a family offered the best chance of the family remaining united. But, a stay in the refugee camp was not to be ruled out. He had returned home thinking he didn't want Mutti to have to experience the camp. She had seemed so terrified of the idea. He had decided would apologize to the Party officials and blame his absence on a nervous breakdown.

He need not have worried about drafting an apology. Party officials fired him immediately. They had been waiting like wolves in hiding to pounce upon a wounded deer. In a document dated December 31, 1954, officials stated that he "stayed away for two days" and that he "violated in the most grievous manner their democratic educational principles."

"What do they know about 'educational principles'?" he stormed, forgetting to whisper. "Where are the educational principles in brainwashing children into Marxist puppets?"

I could feel the wind beginning to nudge my thin tumbleweed body. This time the confrontation with the communist officials did not result in "nothing."

Now unemployed, Vati started sending out application after application for any kind of job. He might as well have spared the ink. He received not a single response. He had not joined the Communist Party and as a result had been blacklisted as a "capitalist sympathizer." People were afraid to be associated with an "anti communist activist."

Mutti found a job in a grocery store where she stayed about six weeks. Her earnings were DM 150 (about $63 at that time) a month. Shortly after that she moved to a fabricated metal plant as an administrative clerk.

This situation drove Vati into despair. German culture of the time was still very much a male dominated society, especially when it came to employment. Sure, women had worked in stores and factories during the war. And after the war able-bodied women outnumbered men by a wide margin. So the cultural norms were giving way to a "reality check." But for a male within a household to be unemployed while his wife was working was a major affront to "human dignity."

The whispers and the planning once again became the routine. The tumbleweed returned to school down the hill in Altoschatz. The same school I had attended before our move to Luppa.

I missed out on most of the whispering. But before spring arrived that year, this nine-year-old tumbleweed began to feel weak around the roots.

A Harrowing Escape

It was 4:00 p.m. on March 15, 1955, when Vati and Mutti came home from the Polizeiamt in Oschatz. They had left Mama's house in Kleinforst earlier to visit the police department in Oschatz. They had decided to try to get permission for legal travel to West Germany. Of course, this was somewhat like asking a prison warden's permission for an unescorted picnic in the woods. On the way to the department Vati became so overwhelmed by panic, they stopped and visited with friends for a couple of hours. It was 1:00 p.m. when they arrived at the police station. There they had to wait for two hours. They felt certain the wait was calculated. They were being observed for signs of anxiety.

"We would like authorization to travel to my brother-in-law's wedding in West Germany," Vati asked the policeman.

"Who would be going? You alone? Or you and your wife?" the man asked.

"We both want to go. We haven't seen him for years. After the war, before he reached home, the French nabbed him. He was sitting in a Gasthaus near Strasburg at the French border, minding his own business." Vati replied. "The damned French drugged him. The next he knew he was aboard some rusty old freighter."

Vati explained that my uncle had recently returned from fighting with the French Foreign Legion in Vietnam. It wasn't just an elaborate story. Mutti's brother had, indeed, been forced into the Legion. He, along with other German men, had been "shanghaied" and had been with the French at the battle of Dien Bien Phu. After the French defeat, Uncle Franz had made it back to Germany.

"He lives near the Black Forest," Vati told the policeman.

"Ach! This is nothing but a ruse. You want to stay in West Germany, don't you?" the police man sarcastically shouted.

"Of course not," Mutti answered. "We have our family and our lives here! This is where our roots are! All we want is to attend my brother's wedding."

"And why does your brother live in the West," the policeman retorted, "if your family's roots are here?"

It was clear the policeman wasn't listening at all. His mind was set that my parents were manufacturing nothing but an excuse to go to the West. He was right, of course, but it helped that the story was true. It made it easier to lie.

"I cannot make any decision at this time. I'll have to discuss this with my superiors. I suggest both of you come back tonight at 7:00 p.m. Then we'll discuss your papers," the policeman had made it sound as if there might be a chance of approval.

Terrified by the ordeal they had walked home faster than usual. My father arrived showing the pain from his artificial leg. My mother's face was grayer than the dusk behind her. Giving us kids barely a glance, they hurried into the house and sat with Mama and Papa at the kitchen table.

"But I was suspicious," Vati was back to whispering at home. And this time water was running in the kitchen sink as he whispered to Mama and Papa.

"I noticed a pink slip of paper attached to our papers as the policeman placed the file on his desk."

"This was a definitely not simply a separator between pages," he said. Panic sharpened his whispered voice and appeared in the taut skin of his reddened face. "When I saw it, I grabbed Mutti by the hand and we rushed out of the office."

"You know what that means," Vati told Mutti's parents now leaning tightly over the table. "The office is closed at 7:00 p.m. The pink slip on our file is the order to arrest us! It's the tactics the damned communists learned from the Nazis. They don't want to make this kind of arrest in daylight. They want us to just quietly disappear into the darkness!"

A deep discussion continued as blue-grey light outside signaled the onset of darkness. It was clear that my parents had no intention of returning to the police station. I pretended to be reading a schoolbook. In that way I overheard most of the urgent whispering. I learned that it was Mama who had hatched the plan calling for my parents to seek a permit to visit my long absent uncle in the black forest.

"Look, Kaethe," Mama said at one point, "With you and Franz living in the West, at least half of my family would be living in freedom. And Papa and I, as you know, will have no trouble joining you."

That remark puzzled the now trembling tumbleweed. It wasn't until years later that I learned why Mama had made it sound so easy for her and Papa to make it to the West while my parents were so filled with fear and constantly whispering about their plans for escape. For Mama and Papa it truly was "no trouble." They were old. Retirees, especially those having earned social security retirement payments, were welcome to leave and go to the West. That way the West, not the East and its communist government, would be paying the elderly their social security benefits. But what does a nine-year-old tumbleweed know about such things?

What I did know was that Vati kept insisting that I should stay in Kleinforst with Mama, and that he, Mutti, and the boys would be going on a trip.

"I can't, Herbert," Mutti cried. "If we do that, we will never see her again. I will take her with me," Mutti said, "and the boys will travel with you!"

They noticed me not reading my book and sent me back outside where my brothers had been re-arranging dirt in

Mama's garden. I sat on the steps and wondered if Hase and Kerndl had any clue that something monumental was about to happen. I wasn't so sure being older was an advantage. I was all shakes and trembles inside. Questions without answers and visions and fears and fragments of conversations were all roiling about. I was hungry but had no appetite. So I watched numbly as two little boys built highways and bridges in the dirt.

A few minutes later Mutti came running out of the house and began brushing the dirt off of our coats.

"We have to leave right now! We're going to visit Uncle Albert, in Eberswalde," Mutti was not whispering. But she was gasping. It seemed as if she could not get enough air to fill her lungs.

Earlier, the discussion had been about Uncle Franz in the West. Now the topic was a younger uncle. I tried to sort it out, but the shakes and trembles ruled.

I did know that Mutti's brother Albert was going to school to become a forester. It was his room that had been commandeered as Mama and Mutti looked on in dismay. The tumbleweed could not decide whether she remembered that day or just the stories about that day. But Albert was still away at school. Eberswalde was located north of Berlin but still within East Germany. I could make no sense of it all. It didn't seem to fit with today's whispers not to mention any other day's whispers.

"But why do we have to go right now?" I asked Mutti.

"I'll explain it to you later. Just don't ask any more questions. We have to leave right now," she huffed.

The slightest hesitation could have meant prison and many years of hardship for my parents. There was only one thing to do and that was to leave. But that was not something the tumbleweed knew at that moment.

Vati came running out of the house carrying a small brief case. Mutti whisper-shouted, "You, Kindl, are going with me, and the boys will go with your father."

What she didn't say was that we would be going on separate trains. But Mutti had called me "Kindl," which was my nickname. It means something like "loving child" if translated to English. What it meant to me that night was that Mutti had settled the question about whether I was to travel with them or remain with Mama and Papa.

"Say good bye to your grandparents," Mutti frantically whispered.

I tried to make sense of which things were whispered and which were not. No luck. Besides, there was no time to dwell on that distinction.

"How could we visit our uncle while we, especially the boys, were still so dirty?" I wondered. "Where were our suitcases?"

More of those questions without answers. Vati carried only a small briefcase. Mutti carried nothing that I could see at that moment. I found out later that she had stuffed the important family documents into her pants.

I couldn't understand why everything had to happen so fast. No one seemed to want to answer my questions.

"I'll miss you Mama," I cried.

"Let's go. We'll miss the train," Mutti whispered. Her face filled with tears, Mama ran back into the house.

"Vati will go to Altoschatz to catch the train from there. You and I will go to the main train station in Oschatz," Mutti briefly explained.

"Why can't we go together," I asked?

"I cannot explain things right now. "Let's go. We don't want to miss our train," Mutti said while she draped a net bag on Kerndl allowing him to carry his favorite teddy bear.

And into the darkness, Vati disappeared with the boys. And the hungry and not hungry went to war in my stomach.

Mutti held my hand very tight as if she were afraid of losing me. Her hands were cold. Her scarf around her neck was lightly loosened to get enough air. I shivered and clutched Mutti's hand anxiously. Would I ever see my father and my two brothers again I thought? The new snow cover seemed to make it even colder. But I felt secure having Mutti by my side no matter what the temperature was. No words were spoken. We just walked and walked as we traveled down old cobblestone streets.

Mutti made it very clear that I was not to talk, not even to ask questions. "People are always listening," she said as she bent to button my jacket. "We can't let anybody know where we are going."

I understood. Sort of. It was dark. We really couldn't see whether there was anybody close to us. And for that reason we couldn't tell if anyone was listening. Besides, I didn't know where we were going. How could I let anybody know?

The 45-minute walk seemed forever. We arrived at the train station just in time to catch the after work train headed towards Leipzig. No sign of Vati and the boys.

In Leipzig, roughly 54 kilometers from Oschatz, we met Vati and the boys at the train station. I was very happy to see them. My parents on the other hand looked more fearful than when we left Kleinforst. It was obvious even to me that this was meeting was not planned. They didn't talk very much. Inside the train station there was a restaurant. But we didn't go in. Vati bought us each a little bread roll with cheese from a shop that had a small window facing the walkway inside the train station. A grumpy looking woman with squinty eyes peered at us as Vati gave her a coin. We had a bite to eat and then Mutti was anxious to leave.

"We'll take the next train to Dessau, and you and the boys can catch the second one," Mutti said to Vati. "That'll be best, won't it?"

I was busy chewing my cheese roll. I wanted to ask why "it was best" but Mutti's quick glance confirmed what I had guessed. The no-talking rule was still in effect.

Mutti and I boarded the last car of the train to Dessau. The door opened up as the conductor was still blowing his final whistle and I felt my eyes pop wide open. Vati and the boys rushed in.

I started to shout, "Vati, Vati," but Mutti's still cold hand immediately covered my mouth. Her face told me to be quiet. Vati walked by without appearing to notice us. He pushed Hase and Kerndl in front of him and found a seat on the cold wooden benches a few rows in front of us.

We had suddenly found ourselves dangerously in the same railroad car. This was precisely what my parents had been trying to avoid. I knew we were trying to stay separate even if I hadn't yet figured out why. There was total silence in the compartment. The only sound heard was the clicking of the track while the old steam engine pulled the train out of the Leipzig train station disappeared into the darkness.

The quietness didn't last very long. In front of our compartment was a train car belonging to the conductor and Vopos. (Peoples' Police). As the train rolled through the darkness we could hear people screaming from inside that compartment.

I broke the no talking rule. "Why are those people screaming? Is someone hurting them?" I asked Mutti.

She didn't respond. The screams stopped after a while. The rhythmic click-clunk of the track began to make me feel more secure. Hase and Kerndl had fallen asleep. Still scared, I cuddled up in my mother's arms. She sat in her seat as if she was frozen. She avoided any eye contact with Vati in order not give any signs that we belonged together. The conductor came but apparently didn't make any connections that we were one family. He checked Vati's train ticket.

"You're going to Strausberg," he commented. Vati nodded signaling with his head that he wished not to awaken the boys.

The conductor continued down the aisle checking tickets and commenting as if the people might not know where they were going.

When he came to Mutti, I heard him clearly, "Sie gehen nach Guestrow."

I stiffened. He had said that my mother was going to Guestrow. I was certain I had heard him tell my father he was going to Strausberg. I felt Mutti pinch my leg.

Mutti, like Vati had done, simply nodded.

"You are traveling one-way," it was a statement, not a question. But the conductor waited for Mutti to respond.

"My sister is ill. It may be some time before I can return."

Now my ears must have become pointed like a pixie. Mutti had no sister.

"You'll have to change trains in Berlin," the conductor said blandly

"Yes, I know, thanks. I make the trip often."

Now I was certain my mother had not told the truth. And that only added to my confusion. It's a strange thing for a child to hear a parent tell a lie. Mutti just told two. She had no sister, and to my knowledge she had never made a trip to a place I had not even heard of. I had no idea where Guestrow was much less why she and I were going there while Vati and my brothers were headed for Strausberg. I thought we were going to Eberswalde to visit her brother as she told me in Kleinforst.

It would be many months before I'd know the truth. And when I did learn the truth, I also learned how close my mother had come to entrapping herself with her "I make the trip often" statement.

Both Strausberg and Guestrow were to the north of East Berlin. The "game plan" my parents had conceived called for them to buy one way tickets to separate destinations. That would make it appear they were not traveling together. Both destinations were located such that to reach them from Oschatz required train changes at Leipzig, at Dessau, and another in East Berlin itself. Changing trains within East Berlin would afford the opportunity to try slipping through checkpoints to reach West Berlin. The tumbleweed did not know that Mutti and Vati had no intention of travelling to either Strausberg or Guestrow. But what I did know was that my mother seemed stiff and frozen, and I had even more of the hungry-but-not-hungry feeling in my stomach.

It seemed to take forever to get to Dessau. The old train couldn't have gone more than 20 miles an hour. We finally arrived at the station around 11:00 p.m. where we needed to catch another train into Berlin. My parents were stricken with fear once again. They were hoping the nightly curfew police would not catch them in the station. A family traveling at night in the direction of Berlin was definitely a sign of escaping. In order to hide us kids they covered us up with their coats to keep us warm and to let us sleep.

It was dead silence in the train station. We were the only ones cuddled together on the cold bench waiting for the next train which was scheduled to arrive at 2 a.m.. The police didn't show up at their usual 12:00 a.m. curfew check.

Punctually at 2:00 a.m. a long train to Berlin rolled into the Dessau station. My parents quickly decided Vati and the boys board the first car while Mutti and I board the last one. As my mother and I entered our car, we noticed only five other women who were already seated in the compartment. They gave Mutti a suspicious look, but no one said a word. They were probably wondering why a mother with young child was traveling so late at night.

Mutti covered me quietly with her coat so I could sleep. I was awakened only once on this leg of the journey. That was when the train stopped for an hour in Schoenefeld on the outskirts of Berlin. This was the pass control point for people entering into East Berlin.

Once again the pass control officials came to check for tickets. Mutti's ticket was for Guestrow, East Germany, which didn't require any additional permission documents. The conductor didn't say anything and apparently didn't see me under the coat. At that time I was awake and was wondering what was going on. The train started to roll again.

Mutti whispered in my ear to quickly look out of the window at the track where hundreds of people stood. These passengers had been removed from the train. Only their silhouettes were noticeable in the dark. Some of them might have later been permitted to continue their journeys.

"See if you can spot Vati and the boys," she whispered into my ear.

She was shaking, terrified that they might be among these passengers who were ordered off the train as suspects of escaping. We could not see whether Vati and the boys were among that group.

The train slowly resumed its creaky forward motion. Mutti and I settled back from the windows. We finally arrived at the Altersbahnhof station in East Berlin. It was early in the morning. People were going to work showing their permission tickets to enter East Berlin to a man who sat in a small hut which was the control point. People had to pass the hut before they could exit the track. The guard spot-checked people for their tickets and occasionally looked down into a book that contained pictures of blacklisted people to see if he could identify someone. Mutti and I stood for a moment to observe what was happening.

"Josefine, I want you to crawl between the people's legs and filter through the crowd. Don't let him see you in the hut. I will follow you. Hurry," Mutti whispered into my ear.

She managed to hide behind a couple of people while walking by the hut. The official didn't notice her or see me ducking between the people. After we made it through she grabbed my hand and both of us hurried to catch the next S-Bahn (above ground train) which was waiting already at the track.

"Is this train going to Friedrichstrasse?" Mutti quickly asked someone.

"No," the person replied.

Just at that moment Vati and the boys ran by and jumped onto the very train we had just avoided. The doors closed, and the train quickly disappeared into the distance.

Mutti let out a quiet sigh. She knew at least that they made it this far and were not among those who were ordered out of the train in Dessau. But she also knew they were on the wrong train. Since Berlin is a major city these city trains (S-Bahn) were frequent and afforded dozens of options for stepping on and off and re-routing.

We waited for the next tram not knowing the exact route, but Mutti knew her goal was to reach the Friedrichstrasse station. That was one of the places from which it was still possible to cross over into the West. Mama had told us that after her ear had been tightly pressed to the radio back in Kleinforst. Vati had used that checkpoint in his earlier trip to the refugee camp in West Berlin. So on we went.

The train was packed with working people. They seemed to stare at us. Were they trying to figure out why a mother and a child were so early in the morning on the train? Mutti made no eye contact with any of them. She was still stricken with fear that a conductor would come asking for the train tickets which of course we didn't have. We had no permission to be in this part of East Berlin. It was off the route to Guestrow, so our tickets were no longer valid.

The crowd became smaller. Most people had exited the train at Friedrichstrasse within East Berlin to go to work. Only a few were left aboard the train. It was absolutely silent in the compartment. We finally arrived at Schoeneberg after an hour's train ride. Schoeneberg was in West Berlin and was the station where Mutti and Vati had arranged to meet. We were the only ones who got off the train. If there was a checkpoint, I couldn't see it. It was 6:00 a.m. The morning was cold and grey. New snow was on the ground. The station was empty. Vati and the boys were nowhere to be seen.

"We are in West Berlin, Josefine," she said. She looked exhausted and pale. She hugged me, her eyes filled with tears. She was heaving and sobbing and trying not to all at the same time.

"We have to find Vati and the boys. I hope they made it. The last time we saw them was at Altersbahnhof. That's where we saw them run by us to catch the train. Let's hurry!" she said.

Mutti's anxiety was evident by her walking so fast that I couldn't keep up. We crossed a wooden bridge which led over the train tracks. Then we could hear a sound.

"Can you hear someone crying?" Mutti asked. "Let's see where it is coming from."

At the bottom of the staircase on the other side of the track near the entrance of the station building we could see three silhouettes sitting on the ground cuddled together.

"Ach, mein Gott!, Here they are!" Mutti shouted before they noticed us.

Kerndl was crying. Vati was shaking with anxiety. She went over to hug him. Torrents of joyous tears washed away the pain of imagined loss, the anxiety, the fear, all of which I shared even without knowing the whole of what we had just done.

"We are finally free!!!!! We made it!!!!! No one can take us back," Mutti cried.

At that point, the tumbleweed began to absorb a truth about those one-way train tickets. Kleinforst and Mama now seemed a thousand miles away. Would I ever see either again?

"I thought you had been arrested since you didn't show up here on time. You are over an hour behind us," Vati said with a scratchy voice. "We thought we would never see you again."

"We also feared that you and the boys might have been arrested after Dessau" Mutti said, "just before crossing the border. They took so many off the train. It was dark. We couldn't see if you might have be among them."

"We were doing the same and couldn't see you either."

"Then we saw you catching the train at Anhalterbahnhof in East Berlin."

"You did? Why didn't you board, too?"

"We were about to enter that same train, but before we did someone told us that it didn't go to Friedrichstrasse."

"Unbelievable!"

"As it turned out, the train we took circled East Berlin before it crossed the border. The people were all going to work."

"It doesn't matter now. We are all together."

The Refugee Camp

Now the inevitable began. Yesterday we had lived in a small village with Mama and Papa. Today we were a homeless family of five on the streets of a city of some 3 million. Both of my parents were unemployed. We had no idea where our next meal would come from, or where we would sleep. We had nothing more than the clothing we wore, and Kerndl's little teddy bear. What Mutti had feared was about to become our reality. But when faced with the inevitable, Mutti was rock solid. She could make the best of anything. Some see a mudslide; Mutti sees new soil for a garden!

We boarded a city bus. After a short ride, we checked ourselves into the refugee camp at Marienfelde. Marienfelde was the first central asylum for refugees from Central Europe and East Germany. There people were provided life's necessities such as food and shelter. The Marienfelde camp consisted of 10 large apartment style buildings. It looked more inviting than what Mutti had feared. We waited for hours in line only to find that Marienfelde was completely booked.

Officials sent us to a makeshift camp near the Tempelhof airport. This camp was an old converted radio factory by the name of Schaub-Lorenz. It had been an industrial building, and it looked cold and uninviting. Instead of keeping us together as a family as would have been the case at Marienfelde, at

Tempelhof, men were separated from women and children. Men stayed on one floor and women and children on another.

Mutti my brothers and I were placed on the third floor in one large open room with 25 other women and children. The bunk beds were so close together that it left very little room to walk. Two large factory windows allowed daylight into the room overlooking the flight path of Tempelhof airport. Kids were constantly crying and women were shouting.

The camp was not an easy place for us. It was the nightmare Mutti had feared. Although we were offered accommodations, received food, water, and other bare necessities, life at the camp was spartan and frightening. The sense of relief my parents had felt in having successfully escaped the East now mixed with feelings of loss and concern about an uncertain future. In this state of mind, they underwent the painstaking routine of the application process in hopes we would be transferred out of Berlin and into West Germany itself, which lay some 120 kilometers further west.

Those papers my mother had stuffed into her clothing proved to be invaluable. We not only had to be able to prove who we were, but we also needed to verify why my parents had fled the communist regime of East Germany.

"Those papers showing why your Vati was fired from his teaching position," Mutti told me years later, "suddenly became good news rather than bad. It was his refusal to teach communist propaganda in the classroom, not the two days of absence, for which he was fired."

We soon came to terms with the strict camp routine, as did the many other residents. The influx to Berlin of refugees much like ourselves created the need for the type of a processing and regimentation we experienced in the Tempelhof refugee camp. Everything was being documented on a dossier called a "Laufzettel" and certified with stamps and initials. This document certified among other things when we received food, hot water and soap for washing. Also Vati's weekly trips to the local authorities where he applied for a political refugee resident permit were documented on this form.

There were always scraping and scratching sounds as people were arriving or leaving each day. One family would disappear, two others would arrive. Metal beds would screech as they were shoved from one place to another. Boxes and crates grated along on the concrete floor. Concrete walls and rusted steel window frames magnified a cacophony of sounds. For the refugees the whole ordeal was an exhausting procedure. The purpose of all the activity was often difficult to understand; at least it was difficult for us children.

Vati told us, "We are just one family, one small part of a massive emigration from the German Democratic Republic."

It would be many years before I truly understood what he was trying to tell us. But the tumbleweed had heard him back in Kleinforst say that East Germany wasn't democratic and wasn't a republic.

"We're all – he was talking about all the refugees at the Tempelhof camp – refugees trying to get into West Germany." Vati told us, "On average the application process normally lasts one to two weeks. For some, it may take longer."

The tumbleweed had a premonition we would be part of that "some" for whom it would be longer.

Although our stay at Tempelhof was precisely the nightmare that Mutti had not wanted to experience, we found ways to make the most of it. We stayed most of the daytime in Vati's room. This room was much larger and had a seating area. On weekends Mutti washed our clothing. She'd wait in line for hot water and then hang the garments overnight at the foot of Vati's bed to dry. The only clothing we had was still what we had worn during our escape.

In our daily refugee camp routine we spent many hours waiting in line for food. The breakfast line began at 6:00 a.m. and though the line remained open until 8:00 a.m., we found it advantageous to be early.

"Wer nicht kommt zur rechten Zeit, der muß essen, was übrigbleibt," Mutti would say to us if we grumbled about getting so early to the line. It was one of those Farmer's Almanac type sayings that grandmas specialize in. This one goes something like, "He who doesn't come at the right time, must eat what is left over." Or the more down to earth, "Early bird gets the worm."

Mutti also taught us to be grateful. "After all, we have left our home, and people at this camp are caring for us," she'd remind us. The food mostly consisted of soups and stews which were poured into our tin cans. Often we moved back to the end of the breakfast line just to wait for lunch.

Vati worked for the camp carpenter shop a few hours a week. For that he earned two Deutsch Marks, which was about 50¢. He also developed cross word puzzles for the Ulstein Verlag, a Berlin publisher who had a shop within walking distance of the Tempelhof camp. When the weather improved, we walked around the neighborhoods and looked into store windows. We saw an abundance of food and other goods, most of which had not been available much less affordable in either Kleinforst or Oschatz. We dreamed about the days when we might be able to buy some of these now so visible goods. Vati was able to buy only a few pieces of chewing gum for us which of course we had never before seen but loved once we were introduced to it.

After three weeks, the paperwork process was coming to an end when I woke up covered with a red rash and a very high fever. At first the camp nurse thought I was allergic to oranges. They placed me in a room in bright sun light for a day's observation. I was burning up. The next thing I can remember was a Swedish nurse in a hospital giving me a cold sponge bath. I had the German measles and a severe case of pneumonia. Across the room another nurse gave a little boy a sponge bath as well.

"What is your name?" my nurse asked.

"Josefine Lohse," I answered.

"Lohse?" the other nurse asked. "I have a boy here by the name of Lohse. Is this your brother?"

"No. I don't know who he is. I haven't seen this boy before," I replied, stricken with fever.

"He has to be your brother," she replied quickly before my nurse hurried me away.

I woke up in a small room with one other patient in a bed next to me. She also was a little girl. I must have been asleep for some time with the high fever. I wanted to say hello but had no voice. She may have not heard me anyway since she was sound asleep suffering from a serious illness. I wanted desperately see my mother but no one came to visit since I was in isolation.

The doctors, according to Mutti, told her to make "arrangements." They were concerned that I might not survive. The pneumonia was too advanced, and the fever didn't seem to break.

I dreamed of an angel sitting at my bedside to whom I often spoke. This angel was my protector. God was trying to save me once again. This was the third time in my short life that I had felt this special protection. The first was when I put my little 16-month-old finger into a wall socket—the scar still noticeable today--and the second time was when I fell headfirst into a six foot water storage tank and almost drowned. Such things happen to most of us. But the tumbleweed had still thousands of miles to wobble, stumble, and roll at the will of winds yet to be encountered. So the angel waited patiently, and in time gave way to Mutti.

Finally, after three weeks I was able to return to the camp. Kerndl had already returned. Mutti told me, "Kerndl was the boy in the hospital you didn't recognize because of your high fever. His stay lasted only a week."

The nurses must have told Mutti about the incident. To me it was all a new story. My other brother, Hase, however, also had come down with the measles and had to be placed in the epidemic ward in another hospital. In addition to his measles his fingernails were swollen and red and secreted pus. He was allergic to Penicillin. It took several days for the doctors to diagnose and treat.

I had not even been aware that both of my brothers had been so ill. So our stay at the Tempelhof refugee camp turned into the nightmare which my mother had been afraid of.

Easter arrived, and we were still waiting to receive our discharge papers. One afternoon, we heard an announcement over the intercom that we had a visitor. Mama had managed to get across the border using much the same route as we had. Of course, she had no idea whether she would find us. Like virtually every household in Kleinforst, Mama had no phone. And my parents knew all mail would be opened and examined, so they hadn't tried to write.

"How did you know where to find us?" cried Mutti. She was overwhelmed with happiness.

We all crowded around Mama like hungry ducks on a pond eagerly snapping up crackers.

"Did Papa come, too?" Mutti asked looking behind Mama.

"No, no," Mama responded. "Papa is home. It's way too risky for us to try now. They're watching us."

"But what about the 'old folks policy'? Has that been repealed already? Vati wanted to know.

"Oh, no, no change there," Mama replied. "But we are under suspicion for helping you. It'll be some time before we can safely apply."

"But you must have had trouble finding us" Mutti again asked.

"Well, I did not know if you had made it safely, but I did know your plans. You were not at Marienfelde, so you had to be here unless you had been captured along the way."

She told us that she had come by train, dressed as an 80-year old woman. No one seemed to bother an old woman. The authorities would not have concerned themselves if she escaped. One less social security benefit to pay, remember?

It was a wonderful reunion, too good to be true to see her again. I missed her so much. Mama brought us additional clothing we had so desperately needed.   She brought us underwear and one featherbed blanket.

She told us that in the morning after our escape, her neighbor had found foot and dog prints in the snow all around Mama's house. The prints led from Mama's house directly to the police station. The neighbor had followed these prints on her way to work that morning. She was afraid that something might have happened to my parents since she was familiar with our situation. She stopped by Mama's house in the evening to tell her what she had seen and learned that we had left the evening before. But Mama, even to a trusted neighbor, revealed nothing except the obvious. We had gone. She truly didn't know of our whereabouts.

After our departure Mama and Papa had been interrogated and tormented. Police and Party officials were furious over our escape. Our departure had made them look inept. So they badgered my grandparents for weeks and years to come.

A few days after Mama's visit, the metallic raspy intercom announced yet another visitor. It was Vati's former colleague who had left Luppa for a teaching position in Strausberg, north of Berlin. That was the very town Vati had applied to teach in. He had been denied the position clearly because he was a thorn in the Communist Party's backside. His colleague apparently had been found more "acceptable" for the job. That alone gave Vati good reason to distrust her. It soon became clear in whose interest she had come. She had been ordered by Party officials to persuade Vati to return to Luppa.

"I was sent to let you know that the Party has forgiven you, and that you should come back," she said.

"Why did they send you?" Vati asked. "Do they expect you to be the Party's negotiator?"

Mutti, my two brothers, and I had crowded close to Vati.

"I'm not at all surprised you got the position. I wasn't suitable, you know. With my dossier? In the town with the Military Headquarters of the German Democratic Republic?"

With that, my tumbleweed ears were alert. Was that sarcasm? Just days ago I had heard Vati say that the GDR was neither democratic nor a republic.

"But you! You are suitable! So it's clear why they've sent you! As their emissary!" Vati was not whispering, I noticed. Not even close to whispering.

"No, Herbert', she used my father's familiar name. "That is not true. They decided to send me because you and I are colleagues, and because Strausberg is near Berlin. Close to Tempelhof," she replied.

Vati could no longer listen to this nonsense. He broke out in a loud laughter. "Who do they think they are kidding? They're asking me to go back to that hell hole? You and I WERE colleagues! Do you think I'm foolish enough to trust either you or them?" Vati's face and neck were red and tense.

"You had better leave now, or I will have you thrown out of this camp," he shouted. Whispering, I concluded, was a thing of the past. But it wasn't. The woman disappeared down concrete steps leading to an exit. I was still close enough to Vati to hear a hoarse whisper. He asked Mutti, "How do you think she knew where to find us?"

Mutti ventured, "Someone might have followed Mama." And Vati added, "Or, there are 'ears' here in the refugee camp!" And the whispering continued.

Leaving the Refuge Camp

The day came when we were finally allowed to leave the refugee camp. The authorities declared that my parents were political refugees. That was an important distinction. Those who were not acknowledged by West Germany as being political refugees, or who had no sponsors in the West, would stay in West Berlin. As political refugees, our family would be permitted to re-locate to West Germany. The State of Rheinland Pfalz had agreed to accept us, as Vati had requested. He had learned our chances of gaining approval would be better in Rheinland Pfalz given that we had no sponsor. Most people asked to be placed in the more industrial areas in Northern Germany in hope of finding work. No one, we were told, who came through the camp was sent back to East Germany. But all of these investigations, certifications, and approvals at federal and state level were the reasons for our long stay in the Tempelhof refugee center. It would be more than 35 years – actually on my 25th wedding anniversary – before the tumbleweed would again see Berlin and the old converted electronics factory. And by that time I would know what a tumbleweed is, and know that I am one. But as we left the refugee center, the tumbleweed had once again that hungry but not-hungry feeling in the depths of my stomach.

We boarded what looked like an old four-engine propeller aircraft at Tempelhof airport. It was the airport from which I had watched the airplanes take off and land while lying on the top of my bunk bed.   I whiled away dreaming that someday I would be on one of those planes. No one in my family seems to remember what type of aircraft it was. It was almost certainly an American plane. No German aircraft were permitted to operate within the Berlin Corridor at that time. Americans operated Tempelhof Airport in those days and flew C-54 cargo planes into and out of Berlin. Some of those were outfitted with seats. In all likelihood that's what it was.

On the flight I remembered the story Mama told me about the Candy Bomber who dropped candies tied to small parachutes from his aircraft to German children during the Berlin Airlift in 1948, about seven years prior to our escape from East Germany. The Berlin airlift had been organized by the Western Allies while I was just a toddler in my East German village. Pilots, mostly Americans, daily carried tons of food and supplies to the people of Berlin. The Soviet Union, which we had seen as tank brigades in Kleinforst, had blocked the Western Allies' railway and road access to the sectors of Berlin under Allied control. This, the Allied Sector, was the part of Berlin we later came to know as free Berlin, or West Berlin. At the time of the airlift, the Russians were trying to use economics to force the western powers out of Berlin. The Russians wanted the Soviet zone to start supplying all of Berlin with food and fuel. This would have given the Soviets practical control over the entire city. In future years the tumbleweed would learn that the United States Air Force, British Royal Air Force, and other allied nations flew over 200,000 flights during the Berlin Airlift which lasted about a year-and-half.

Later in my life, quite by chance, I met Colonel Gail Halverson at the Dallas, TX, airport. It was he who had started dropping candy out of his plane as he was landing his transport plane at Tempelhof. I first heard of him by way of Mama, whose ears, pressed tightly to that forbidden radio in Kleinforst, had gotten word of an American pilot dropping candy and chewing gum to children watching the planes land at Tempelhof. Halvorsen had promised some children he met at the fence surrounding the base that he would wiggle the wings to identify himself. This led to his nickname "Onkel Wackelflügel" ("Uncle Wiggly Wings"). Once his idea took hold, other American candy bombers became known as the Rosinenbombers (Raisin Bombers).

Meeting Colonel Halverson, I remembered being in that cozy Kleinforst kitchen and hearing Mama telling Papa about the Candy Bomber after I was old enough to understand.

"These are the same pilots who three years ago were dropping bombs all over Germany. And now they're dropping candy to our children and feeding the whole city of Berlin!"

So there I was, a mid-fifties woman sitting right next to the Candy Bomber! I was headed for a trade show where I would represent the U.S. Department of Commerce. Colonel Halverson was on his way to Dallas for a presentation about the Berlin Airlift, which had been the highlight of his career. And it so happened that we shared the same limo to the hotel.

His eyes opened wide when I told him I had been a little German girl at Tempelhof, in a refugee camp. We were stuck in traffic for nearly half an hour. It was probably the only time in my life my German blood didn't rattle my bones with impatience while I was stuck in traffic. We talked at length about his exploits in the Berlin Airlift, and my experiences at Tempelhof. Before his departure, he gave me his autograph which I placed on my Hummel airlift figurine that I brought back from Germany on one of my trips.

But now aboard an American airplane roaring and lifting off from Tempelhof, my experiences at the refugee center disappeared into the distance as the tumbleweed was more or less literally blown and lifted into the sky. It was, of course, a first for all of my family.

One other refugee family was on board our aircraft. The rest were regular citizens. The pilot greeted us as guests of the Senate instead of as refugees. This made us feel very special. No one knew that Vati had only one Deutsch Mark (valued at about 25¢ in American currency) and one fountain pen in his pocket.

The non-pressurized flight was rough and noisy from the sound of the propellers. I was afraid of the turbulence we experienced but Vati assured me that it would be okay. It didn't occur to me to ask how he knew that since it was also his first flight.

He added, "We are flying through the air corridor which means that the aircraft must remain in that corridor until we are out of East Germany. That's why we cannot avoid a certain amount of turbulence." Actually, Vati had learned this only moments earlier from the flight attendant while Mutti was strapping us kids in with seatbelts. It would be many years before I would learn the full significance of those corridors, and have it all clearly explained by the Candy Bomber himself.

"See it as an invisible tunnel through the air," Vati explained. "We cannot change our altitude or flight path."

From Halvorsen I later learned that if the pilot did not remain within that corridor, or air tunnel, he could get shot down by the Soviets. That very thing happened a number of times during what later would be called the Cold War.

Vati comforted us by adding, "The pilot knows what he is doing so don't worry. Look out of the window and enjoy the flight." He certainly didn't need to encourage me to look out the window. The scenery below was breath taking. As everything became smaller and smaller, I wondered if I'd be able to see Mama and Papa in Kleinforst.

The flight attendants brought us pretzels and bananas and a drink. I had never before eaten bananas and was surprised by their texture and taste but couldn't understand why monkeys liked them so much. I sure didn't.

We landed safely in the West at Frankfurt and were transported to a quarantine camp in Osthofen near Worms on the Rhein River. We were quarantined not because we had come from East Germany, but because we had come from a crowded refugee camp. At Tempelhof, my brothers and I were not the only refugees who had become ill. Many others had been struggling with a variety of diseases. So our stay at Osthofen afforded doctors an opportunity to monitor our health before we re-located to our new home farther west in the state of Rheinland Pfalz.

The Osthofen camp was quite different. We had one private room for our family and there was plenty to eat. The spring weather was already pretty warm so we could go for daily walks and discover new surroundings. Osthofen is in the midst of Germany's Rheinland wine growing district. It was a small town of farmers, mostly vintners. It is within walking distance of the west bank of the Rhein River, and a few miles north of Worms. The area looked nothing like Saxony and Kleinforst. It seemed all I could see in any direction was grape vines. But we were together, and warm, and had good meals.

The tumbleweed did not have time to sink roots during the brief Osthofen stay, and I remember little of our stay there except that it was a time of contentment, at least for me, and for my brothers. There was no whispering, and at least outwardly Vati and Mutti seemed calm.

At Osthofen we were also provided donated clothing. This we desperately needed. For several months we each had only one item to wear and one for change, even after my grandmother brought us one set each while we were in the refugee camp in Berlin. After a two-week stay and undergoing physical examinations we were allowed to leave for our final destination. Winds of change began to nudge the tumbleweed back into motion.

New Beginnings

Our new lives began as we climbed into the back of a furniture truck carrying stoves, beds, chairs and tables, and three families. It was a large delivery truck without windows. We sat in total darkness on benches along the sides. It felt like a trip to the unknown. My brothers and I were strangely calm in the dark. Maybe because we could feel our parents, and they were calm. The first time the truck stopped and opened the rear doors we were blinded by the daylight. One of the drivers called the name of a family and helped them to step out. The driver unloaded a stove, a hutch, a table and chairs for everyone in that family. The door shut until the next stop.

In the meantime we started to ask our parents if we would be the next ones, and where they were taking us. Oh, yes, little German children, like their American counterparts, are known to ask the proverbial question, "Are we there yet?" It all seemed like a mystery. I had none of the hungry but not hungry feeling in my stomach. Somehow I felt whatever this unknown world was about to reveal, it would be good. Sitting in the dark, feeling the gentle swaying motions of the truck winding itself up hills, then down again, I tried to imagine what our new home would look like. Soon the truck braked and stopped once again. The second family was taken. Once that family had off-loaded, no furniture was left in the truck, only the five of us. This time Mutti spoke to the driver.

"Could you please tell us where we are?"

"In the county of Simmern," he answered.

Simmern didn't mean much to Mutti or Vati since they had never before heard of the county. They could only guess from the terrain they briefly saw when the other families were taken from the truck that we were somewhere in a low mountain range. Maybe it was in the Westerwald, the Eifel, or the Hunsrueck. These were forested areas of Germany's state of Rheinland Pfalz they had seen only on maps. They had thought of the Hunsrueck last since that was known to be the poorest region of Germany. We finally arrived at our destination. It was evening.

"This is the last destination on my route and your new address," the driver said, as he was helping us out.

"Why don't we get any furniture?" I asked. "Can't tell you child," he responded and climbed back into the truck and drove away.

We stood in front of a three story building. The exterior of the building was protected from the weather with gray slate tiles, commonly used in that area of Germany, but starkly different from any home or building I had seen in Kleinforst. That, alone, told me we were in a new land. The tiles on the buildings' sides were mounted in the overlapping fashion of roof tiles. I had the odd feeling that these people didn't know the difference between a roof and a wall.

Several people had been standing around waiting for our arrival. We were expected. A man walked towards us and greeted us.

"Wilkommen to Wohnroth. I am the mayor of the village. We've been waiting for you for a couple of hours," he said. "That truck driver must not be familiar with the Hunsrueck."

"Oh, he seemed to know his way around," Vati responded, "but we weren't his only passengers."

A few pleasantries followed. There were handshakes, greetings and introductions all around. Then the mayor pointed to the upper level of the village schoolhouse.

"Let me take you to your new apartment. It's located on the third floor of our school building. The first floor has the classroom the second is the teacher's apartment. We currently don't have a new teacher, but expect one soon," he continued. This seemed confusing to me until I later learned that Vati – although he was a teacher in East Germany – did not have proper certification for West Germany. That was why we were given the third floor apartment. This was to be a temporary arrangement. The tumbleweed, having snagged onto a new fencepost, apparently would not be taking root here.

We climbed up to the third floor and saw to our surprise that the apartment was furnished with the essential furniture. There were beds and blankets, a kitchen table and a small hutch that contained a few dishes. A stand-alone iron oven with firewood and coal was ready to be lit. A bucket full of potatoes and fresh bread and butter were placed on the table.

"The furniture and essentials have been donated by the local Church," the mayor told us. "The bread, butter, and potatoes were brought in by our village farmers. You are our first refugees, and we want to welcome you to our community. I hope you will like it here," the Mayor continued, as he handed Vati DM70 (seventy West German marks – about 18 dollars) for groceries and then he left.

"I can't believe this. I thought we wouldn't have anything," Mutti cried for joy.

These necessary items were of greater worth than we just weeks ago might have imagined. We had completed an arduous, high risk journey. We had left behind in Kleinforst everything – clothing, household items, furniture, and most of all, Mama and Papa. We arrived in Wohnroth free of the communists who had made our lives miserable. Yet the road ahead of us would be one of privation and struggle. Still, we were happy with what we had just received and were looking forward to our new lives in freedom. The hardships that were ahead of us didn't seem to matter at this time.

Wohnroth was a small village having just 150 inhabitants. It was a suitable place, I see now, for me to land. For like the tumbleweed, this village had been tossed about by the whims of history. It was first mentioned in 1220 by the Trier Archdiocese. At that time it would have been part of the Holy Roman Empire as was most of what today we call Germany. The village became French in 1794 owing to occupation of the French Revolution troops who won control of the left side of the Rhein River. Then, in 1814 Wohnroth became part of the Prussian Kingdom when the Vienna Congress reorganized its territories. Then, not long before our arrival, the village had become part of the newly established State of Rheinland Pfalz. This had happened in post-war 1947 while back in Kleinforst Mutti and Vati were just beginning to come to grips with the aftermath of war as Communists replaced Nazi local leadership.

The tumbleweed did not know all of this on that late spring day when we climbed out of the darkness of that rumbling truck. What I did know was that we had arrived at a place we could call home. At least for a while.

From windows of our three-room apartment, we were able to overlook sloping meadows leading gently toward a picturesque valley known locally as Wohnrother Tal. As we began to explore, we found a small creek running through the narrow valley for about four miles. This led us to the ruins of the castle Balduinseck. There were no connecting roads to the valley except the walking paths which ran parallel to the creek. These paths led to the next village, Bell, on top of a hill. Small mills were nestled between the brush of old oak and beech trees. All of this had made the valley a historical vacation destination.

New challenges began for us right away. The poverty and chronic chaotic conditions of our first year in freedom have left a lasting impression on me for years to come. In the fall of 1955 Vati's unemployment check came to an end. He wondered if they had made the right decisions to come to the State of Rheinland Pfalz instead of northern Germany's industrial region where a greater number and variety of jobs might be available.

"I don't know what else to do. I am at the end of my rope. We need money for food," Vati said to Mutti. "I am not allowed to teach in West Germany without the proper West German credentials."

Mutti listened patiently while Vati continued.

"Now we are stuck in this small village and have no way of getting out of here," he added.

Mutti waited a moment before speaking.

"Why don't you contact Ms. Wilke, your former colleague from Altoschatz? Doesn't she now live here in the West, in Heidelberg? Remember she was one of the teachers they fired after our Mardi Gras party. She left for West

Germany soon after. Perhaps she'll have some advice for you on how to get your credentials here in the West," Mutti answered.

In a rare display of humility, Vati asked, "Why didn't I think about that. This is a great idea. I'll do it right away," he replied.

Within a short time, Ms. Wilke responded and provided contact information at the Teachers Academy in Worms and suggested he apply for schooling. He followed her recommendation.

After sending his application, Vati visited the post office every morning to check on the mail. He was too anxious to wait until the mail was delivered to the house. He told Mr. Leonhard, the post man, that he was desperately waiting for a letter from Worms. One day when I was with my parents looking for firewood in the nearby forest close to the main route into the village, Mr. Leonhard drove by. He had just picked up the mail from the main post office in nearby Kastellaun.

"I believe you have received a response you were waiting for, Mr. Lohse," he said waiving a letter in his hands.

Nervously Vati opened the letter and broke out in a joyful scream. "They accepted me!"

We hurried up with the firewood, loaded everything on our small hand-held wagon and rushed home.

It was February 1956. The letter stated that he was accepted and should report to school on April 1st for a two-year teacher certification program. He was spared the school entry exam because he had taught for several years in the past.   It was just in the nick of time, since the cut-off age for individuals was 33, and he was 32 years old. The good news was beginning to look promising. My parents were able to see a glimpse of light at the end of the tunnel and were dreaming of better times.

The reality, however, set in quickly.   There was no money for books or for new clothing. The State of Rheinland Pfalz government offered to pay only his tuition.   In return for that he would be required to serve as a teacher for five years within that State.   In desperation Vati took a trip to Bell to our local pastor and explained the situation.

"Mr. Lohse, our parish will help you. Let me find out what we can do for you, and I will let you know next Sunday what we've decided," the pastor answered trying to calm Vati down.

On the following Sunday the pastor reported that the Church agreed to pay for room and board and provide donated clothing.   Vati was so overwhelmed with this offer. Although joyful that this opportunity was given to him, he experienced anxiety as to whether or not he could fulfill his commitment. He was about to enter a Teacher's Academy where the students were graduates from local Gymnasiums, students with credentials my father didn't have. It would mean that he would have to work twice as hard to gain his certification.

April came and Vati was off to Worms. Mutti, my brothers, and I stayed behind in Wohnroth scraping along in survival mode in our newly found village in the Hunsrueck. Mutti received a welfare check of DM 12 ($3) per week which barely covered food expenses. In the summer she worked for the local farmers who paid DM 2 per day (about 50¢) but they also provided breakfast and lunch. The small farms brought in just enough money for their own survival, and therefore, were not able to pay more. After all it had been only 10 years since World War II ended, so the whole economy still struggled for recovery.

The Wohnroth farmers' fields were very small and each farmer's plots were scattered within a two mile radius around the village. The harvesting techniques they used were very primitive. No one at that time in the village had a tractor. Instead they used oxen to plow the fields and to pull their wagons for harvesting, or fertilizing.

When not in school during the summer, we would accompany Mutti and the farmers to the fields. Our trips to the fields started early in the morning and finished late in the afternoon. We'd get back to the village just in time to help feed the livestock and milk the cows. Growing and harvesting the village's small-grain crops was backbreaking work. Virtually every morsel of what was harvested was touched by hand. The farmers cut their grain by hand with a sickle, bundled the cuttings into sheaves, stacked these in shocks to dry, and then took the dried product to the threshing machine in the barn.

My brothers and I held up the grain sheaves so Mutti could stack the shocks. We usually made a game out of this and sometimes used the shocks as hide-and-seek places. The best time in the fields was when we had lunch and snacks in the afternoon. The farmer's wife would bring freshly baked bread, homemade butter and smoked ham, as well as cakes for the later afternoon break. This was a real treat for us, and therefore, we didn't mind working hard in the fields. So, the tumbleweed took root and sprouted during these years of hard work and learning.

One day I watched Mutti as she taught a village farmer a better way to load a wagon with the dried sheaves. She noticed that his wagon was lop-sided and ready to fall. She'd take the sheaves, handed to her by him with a pick fork, and laid them on two sides along the edge of the wagon with the grain facing the middle. She then placed several sheaves lengthwise in the middle of the rows in order to hold them down. She repeated that about 10-12 times until the wagon was loaded high and, of course, straight. This was back-breaking work normally done by males. The farmer was so surprised that a city-slicker knew how to perform that task. He didn't know that only a few years before coming to Wohnroth Mutti had worked in the fields of the agricultural manors in East Germany. It was there during the summers where she had observed this skill.

Thrashing in the barn was another dusty and dirty job. We'd collect the grain in burlap sacks, and stack the remaining straw in the barn. There it would be used in the stalls where it would collect cow droppings. This aromatic mixture of dung and straw they'd then neatly stack in front of the barn. Later in the fall this would be used for fertilization in the fields. The higher the cow pile, the richer the farmer. It showed that he had several cows in his stall. The village farmers kept their dairy cows in stalls due to a lack of grazing land. The milk brought in additional money. The cows were milked by hand in the evenings and in the mornings. Early in the morning, one village farmer collected the milk cans and delivered them to the nearby dairy, about 3 miles from Wohnroth.

The hay that fed the cows throughout the year was piled up loosely in the barn. There were no machines available that bundled the hay into rolls. So the farmers would mow the field grass with a hand scythe and arrange it in rows. These had to be turned over with a fork or a rake for the sun and wind to dry. The more often they turned the grass the faster it dried. Once dried, they'd stack the hay on the wagon and take it to the barn. So, the tumbleweed and her little brothers learned and practiced village farming techniques that dated back to the

Middle Ages while Vati was away pursuing his teaching certification.

After a year's vacancy Wohnroth's new school teacher finally arrived and moved into the school house apartment below us. We no longer had to walk through winter's ice and snow to the next village to attend school. It was a treat just to walk downstairs. That, however, didn't last. Mutti realized we were an imposition upon the new teacher and his family, so she decided to move into a one-hundred-year-old farm house just down the street. There, we occupied three rooms upstairs. The ceilings were very low, the windows small and the wooden floors old and dry. The few donated furniture that we had received were just enough to fill the rooms. The boys slept on their straw mattresses in one bedroom while I had my own. My room was large enough to hold one small bed. There was no heat in those rooms. Mutti heated up large volcanic rocks in the oven and warmed our beds with them before we climbed in. The kitchen had a cast-iron wood-burning stove which we kept clean with a steel pad after each use keeping the chromed steel top shiny. Every morning after we got up we took turns making the fire by placing small sticks in the burning unit to start the fire. We'd keep it going all day during winter months. This was our cooking stove as well as a heater for keeping the room warm. A small sofa, a well-worn wooden table with four chairs and a small cabinet for dishes made up our kitchen, which did double duty as family room and living room. The window overlooked the main street with farm houses on both sides of the street.

Mutti raised rabbits she kept in small stalls next to the house. Rabbit was a delicacy for a Sunday meal while during the week our main nourishment was potatoes, milk soup, vegetables and noodles. Mutti received here and there some food from the farmers where she worked. Twice a week the baker arrived on his horse-pulled wagon from a neighboring village to deliver breads and bread rolls. He was a good man and usually gave my brother Hase some left-over bread. The baker was particularly fond of him. The local church provided us U.S. Care packages with dried milk powder and cheddar cheese.

The entire village and its surroundings were our playgrounds. In the summer we climbed fruit trees and stuffed our tummies with cherries, apples and plums. In the fall we stuffed ourselves with potatoes that were steamed in a large potato steamer. The steamer was rented by the farmers for a week so they could steam their potatoes. These they kept in an underground silo to be used for pig food. We loved to climb on the machine which was parked in the middle of the village. We'd eat the freshly steamed potatoes right from the cooker. In the summer after school, we took trips into the woods and collected fire wood. The woods were filled with dead tree limbs lying on the ground. We'd break these into pieces and stack them on our small hand-held wagon. These limb pieces were our only fuel for cooking and heating since we had no money for coal. Neatly we stacked our gathered wood behind the house for the winter months to come.   In August we picked berries. There were plenty of wild berries growing along the edges of the woods. With a small tin can we made our way through the thorny bushes harvesting raspberries and blackberries from which Mutti made jelly for the winter. She could not go with us on these berry-picking trips since she worked for a farmer harvesting grain and vegetables. She came home at night exhausted and in lot of pain from the heavy work.

Between our trips to the woods, I babysat for the village's only local grocer who also was a farmer. His small grocery store was usually closed during the day while he was out in the fields. I stayed home with their baby. Once in a while a customer would come seeking an urgent food item. I'd unlock the store, sell her the item and immediately lock up again. It was very tempting to reach into the candy jar while no one was watching, but my upbringing and my belief in the 10 Commandments kept me from doing so.

Mutti received an old foot-pedal-powered sewing machine from a farmer. This she used in the winter months to sew clothing for us. She took apart old adult clothing which had been donated by the local Church, and using that cloth she'd make something new for us. Occasionally she earned a little extra money by sewing dresses for local women.

After the first year of Vati's schooling in Worms, I was of age to attend what Germans call high school, or Gymnasium. In Germany this was grades 5 through 13. Kids who planned to learn a trade would stay in the elementary school track. Others who had good grades and wanted higher education went on to Gymnasium and eventually attend a university. The nearest high school was located in Simmern and was reachable only by train from the nearby village of Bell. The distance was roughly 20 km. Wohnroth had no public transportation which meant that I would have to walk early in the morning through a wooded valley to the train station in Bell, about 3 km. Then catch a train to Simmern and take a commercial bus to school. My parents did not consider this a good option and decided instead that I would go with Vati to Worms and attend the Eleonore-Gymnasium there. The tumbleweed was once again in motion.

Vati arranged for me to stay with one of his colleague's family who was living in a small apartment in Worms. Soon after the arrangement was made, and I started school, the man's wife developed tuberculosis which resulted in me having to move out immediately. Vati was devastated. He had no idea what to do with me. I couldn't stay in his dorm. I couldn't continue my education back in Wohnroth. A nearby children's foster home run by Lutheran nuns turned out to be the solution.

The three-story home had approximately 30 children many of whom had been mistreated by their parents or had been orphaned. The home was located reasonably close to Vati's school on the outskirts of the city. Mutti paid for my room and board from the little welfare money she received. In the mornings I took a bus into the city and attended school. Afternoons I often stopped by Vati's dorm to do my homework. It seemed to work out pretty well. I actually liked the home except when the social workers brought in another child who had been abused. I almost fainted when a three-year old boy arrived whose mother had placed a hot frying pan on his head and burned his skull. He was still covered with bandages on his head.

I was allowed to stay in a special bedroom with a girl named Dagmar who quickly became my best friend. Her 80-year-old grandmother stayed in a local nursing home where we frequently visited her. Dagmar's mother was a prostitute in Munich and was not able to raise her.

The nuns were lot of fun. I spent many afternoons with Sister Mary helping her in the kitchen. She was the cook. Sister Gerda was the strict one and the best story teller. She read us stories every night after dinner. Sister Helena showed us how to have fun. Her laughter could be heard throughout the house.

Mother Katharina, our superior mother, kept everybody in line. I have few memories of school life in Worms, except that I was an outsider. Most of the other students had grown up together, shared experiences, and had long ago formed friendship groups of which I was not a part. I was called "the Flüchtlinge" (the refugee), and that was all that anybody seemed to want to know about me. This, it turns out, would be an often repeated scenario in my life, both personal and professional. After all, who makes a houseplant out of a windblown, crispy and thorny-looking tumbleweed?

Still, my stay in Worms did have its highlights. For example, during Christmas the U.S. Army Enlisted Wives in Worms brought us to their Noncom Club for a Christmas party. I was proud to be able to speak 100 words of English which I had learned in school. I was mesmerized by these Americans. They seemed so friendly and smiled a lot. The energy of generosity was felt throughout the room. We watched a Donald Duck movie, and another called the City and the Country Mouse. We ate as much cake and candy as we wanted. To my surprise, I even received the very gift I had asked for which was an umbrella. After the party I dreamed many times about going to America some day and see the country where these wonderful women came from. Little did I know that a huge but friendly wind would blow this little tumbleweed all the way across the Atlantic Ocean and fulfill that very dream.

Several years after my stay in the foster home, I learned that my second cousins, who came from Poland, also found refuge in Worms. Their father, an uncle on my mother's side, had escaped across the border without his family, and later, with the help of the Pope, he was able to bring his family out of Poland. Since his children didn't speak any German, they attended a German language school in Worms and stayed in the very same foster home where I had been. The sisters mentioned to them that years before they had a little girl staying with them. Her name was Josefine who was enjoyed and loved by all sisters. To their surprise they found out that I was one of their cousins. Today I have two nun figurines in my curio cabinet that resemble two of the three sisters. These sisters will always have a special place in my heart, as I apparently had in theirs.

Life in the Hirschfeld Village

In April of 1958 Vati graduated and received his West German teaching credentials. I finished my first high school year at the Eleonore Gymnasium at the same time. Vati was now committed to teach five years for the State of Rheinland Pfalz in order to pay back what the State had spent on his two-year education. He received his first new assignment in a small village called Hirschfeld, some 20km west of Wohnroth. The tumbleweed once again succumbed to the winds of change. My Kleinforst home and Mama and Papa seemed ever so distant. In this new village, and soon in yet another new school, I would remain "der Flüchtling," a refugee, an outsider. The villagers called themselves "Hirschfelder" as in "those of Hirschfeld." I would never be a Hirschfelder. To this backward, hill-country village of farmers to whom inside plumbing was considered futuristic, I would be, and would remain, a curiosity, an anomaly.

Hirschfeld was connected to the Hunsrueck Hoehenstrasse, which was a state highway built during the war years. It was a "modern" highway connecting Koblenz on the Rhein River with Trier on the Mosel River. The area was called the Hunsrueck, a very scenic part of the state of Rheinland Pfalz, about 50 km west of Frankfurt. Rolling hills surrounded the village with the highest mountain, Idar Kopf, about 350m.

The village had approximately 300 inhabitants, mostly farmers. Unlike Wohnroth where the people were all Lutherans, Hirschfeld was one third Catholics and two thirds Protestants. This demographic divide would play a role as the tumbleweed struggled to put down roots.

The school house was new, in fact was one of the newest structures in the village. It was located at the village entrance at the crest of a gentle hill. This, too, played a role in my lack of social acceptability. The schoolhouse, built at taxpayer expense, had been designed and built with "the latest" in indoor plumbing and electricity. Some of the village homes – some structures as old as 200 years – had such conveniences only as added features. As a result, many of the villagers looked upon us with envy. We were, in their eyes, the privileged class.

The school building had two classrooms and an office for Vati located on the first floor. The second floor was our apartment with three bedrooms, a large living room, a kitchen and a bathroom. It was, for us, our dream house, large, light filled, and airy. On one side of the house was a fenced-in vegetable garden for Mutti to tend. In the basement was the public bathing area where villagers could come on Saturdays and take their weekly bath. Not everybody had a bathroom with a tub or shower inside their house, and bathing was only done on weekends. There were also freezer compartments in the basement available for locals to keep their frozen foods. So the schoolhouse was much more than simply classroom space. It was home, school, and community facility all in one. What the villagers did not likely know: we were still living with donated furniture, donated clothing, and had but a few coins to our name. Yet, to me it seemed we didn't need anything else. We have it all I thought: a beautiful place to live, and of course Vati had a job. He was the village teacher and would be teaching as many as 30 children grades 1-8 in two classrooms.

It was an overwhelming challenge that he didn't quite expect. He would work with students of one group for 20 minutes while the other students had quiet assignments. Then he switched to the next group. At 1:00 p.m. every day he'd come upstairs for lunch totally exhausted. After lunch he'd take a short nap then return downstairs to his office to prepare for the next day. After a break for dinner he'd return to his office until late in the evening. This was his daily routine.

Money was still short and food was still scarce. Mutti had DM5 ($1.25) per day for groceries which made it very difficult to feed a family of four. She would often send me to the local store to get food on credit. I hated to shop on credit, knowing that she couldn't pay it back. Every time the grocer took his small book out of the drawer to enter our grocery bill I would get a stomach ache. I was embarrassed as a teacher's daughter to have to go shopping on a credit. I thought such things would only apply to poor people. I don't even know to this date if any of the local farmers were listed in that little black book.

One day while I shopped, the old man grocer came to me and said, "Tell you parents that I have erased the entire owed balance from my books. It has been three months since your parents made any payments, and I doubt that they will be able to do so."

"OK Mr. Bart. I will tell my mother right away. You are a very kind man. My parents will appreciate this very much," I replied as I stormed out of the store.

"Mutti, Mr. Bart destroyed our page in the black book," I shouted entering the kitchen.

"Why did he do that?" she asked.

"I don't know. He just did."

"There are still good people in the world," she continued. "We are still having such a hard time to make ends meet. You know that we had to leave everything behind in East Germany and have had to start from the beginning."

I certainly didn't need to be told that we had left everything behind. I had not forgotten the Berlin refugee camp, and memories of the Wohnroth farming village were still fresh. But I surely was not ready for the next thing Mutti said.

"I also must tell you that I am having another baby."

"What another baby?" Why? I am already 13, and now you are having another baby?"

"We can't make it with the five of us? And now we will be six?" I cried.

Totally embarrassed I walked into my room. It had never occurred to me that my parents actually still "did it."

Not getting a meal at the school, my daily intake of food consisted of a piece of bread with jelly at breakfast, another jelly bread at 10:00 a.m. during our school break, and a cold left-over lunch at home, normally the Germans' main meal. This I ate around 2:00 p.m. after returning home from my classes at a high school quite some distance from our home in Hirschfeld. Most lunches included potatoes and some sort of gravy or pasta. Meat was a Sunday treat. At night we had a sandwich with cheese or lunch meat. It was an utter race with my brothers to the table to see who would get the best piece. The lack of good nutrition soon played a role in my grades at school. I had turned into a mediocre student compared with my performance at the school in Worms. I seemed always to have trouble to concentrate and comprehend. It puzzled my home room teacher since according to him I was an intelligent child. He couldn't understand why I wasn't performing based on my abilities. He didn't know that I was too embarrassed to tell him about my situation at home.

Baby Bübchen was finally born in May of 1959, one year after we moved to Hirschfeld. That fall Mutti continued teaching home economics in the afternoons in the surrounding villages to make ends meet. I was in charge of watching my baby brother and my other two brothers after I returned from my school. This left little time for my homework which I had to finish late at night, if at all. There were occasions when I needed help with my homework, but Vati was too tired to help me out. I tried hard to understand the situation that our family was in, but I felt very alone. I don't remember that my mother ever sat down with me just to talk. The words "I love you" never were said. Yes, I knew they loved me in their own way. They provided for me.

Every Sunday I attended the Lutheran Church while I was in confirmation classes. Pastors came from neighboring villages each week to Hirschfeld for Sunday worship services. The Catholics would attend their service in their church on one side of the village, and the Lutherans attended theirs in their church on the other side of the village. This set-up made evident a precise separation between the people based on their religions. The villagers tolerated each other, but sometimes that was the extent of it. Mixed-religion marriages were not approved by the elders. Such was village life in Hirschfeld.

But a more aromatic custom of village life came each Saturday morning. This was when the village women baked their breads and cakes in an old "Backhaus" (baking house) that was located in the middle of the village. A calendar on the wall indicated who was responsible for building the fire inside the two brick ovens and who was responsible for cleaning up. The burning fire gave off the heat which the heavy oven walls absorbed. Once the dome chamber inside was heated to flat white-hot, the fire was allowed to die down or kept burning very gently. Then breads and cakes were placed on a long wooden spatula and pushed into the ovens. This low tech system baked the best tasting breads and cakes imaginable. A wonderful aroma spread throughout the village. Everyone knew it was Saturday. The villagers baked large sheets of fruit cakes for use throughout the whole week and, of course, for the Sunday afternoon visits. The tradition was to eat cake and drink coffee around 3:30 p.m. when visitors stopped by for a Sunday afternoon chat. German cakes are usually not very sweet, and are sometimes an alternate for bread.

One of the best times I remember was when the village boys used the Backhaus for their first May Day prank. May 1st is the German Labor Day and a holiday. It is also the day when the ancient traditional Maibaum (Maypole) is raised in the middle of the village to welcome spring, and the village kids carry out their pranks during the night before. A Maibaum is a tall wooden pole made from a tree trunk. A spring wreath is placed atop the Maibaum with colorful ribbons, flowers, carved figures, and various other decorations adorning it, depending on the location in Germany. That particular night the boys disassembled a farm wagon that is usually pulled by oxen or tractors and reassembled it inside the Backhaus. This prank was kept quiet until the women came to bake their bread the following Saturday.

The farmers in Hirschfeld were small farmers. The average farmer had four milk cows, some pigs and chickens and usually a large vegetable garden. The size of their fields was about 5-10 hectares which were scattered on the outskirts of the village. A few farmers owned by then a tractor while others still used oxen or cows to pull their wagons. The milk cows were kept in the stall year round. Their dung was piled high in front of the barn. The pile was stacked perfectly straight using layers of straw as had been done in Wohnroth. The motto was, the higher the pile, the richer the farmer. In the fall the dung and sewage would be carted to the fields and used as fertilizer. At that time of year the "honey wagon'" odors overwhelmed the Saturday aroma from the Backhaus.

Our family, being the teacher family, lived in a "glass house." In order to keep our father's reputation intact, our parents expected us to set the standards for the rest of the village kids. We knew my father's rules and the consequences if these rules were broken. Such expectations are not unlike those experienced by kids anywhere whose parents are preachers or teachers. But when combined with being a refugee, an outsider, and one whose language seemed too formal to ears accustomed to the local dialect, striving to meet Vati's expectations gave me reputation of holding myself aloof of the village kids. The outsider syndrome must have been stamped on my forehead.

Another factor limiting my contact with the local kids was the fact that there was no high school in Hirschfeld. My father's school kept most of the village kids in elementary school for eight years. After that, those students could go on to learn a trade. Since I had already completed one year of Gymnasium in Worms, my parents had signed me up in a high school in Traben-Trarbach, a Mosel River town 10 kilometers from Hirschfeld. That, too, separated me from the village kids, very few of whom were destined for either high school or university. I left the village every morning on foot. In order to get to school, I walked one mile to the Hunsrueck Hoehenstrasse to catch a public transportation bus which usually arrived at 7:00 a.m. The Hunsrueck Hoehenstrasse was a brand new main highway connecting Koblenz and Trier. That road alone was something that held most of the villagers in awe since it was the connection to the "outside world."

My bus ride took about 45 minutes to Traben-Trarbach which is located in the famous wine growing valley of the Mosel River. The serpentine and steep narrow roads that led to river banks below and to the city were a daily challenge for our bus driver. In winter navigating this road was a hazardous task.

From the bus station in Traben-Trarbach, I walked another mile to reach the school. School was out at 1:00 p.m.

early enough for me to catch the bus home. I arrived at home usually around 2:30 p.m. after walking one mile from the bus station back to the house. The winters were harsh. We didn't have snow days. No matter how bad the weather was I had to go on my daily trips to school. I recall experiencing several snow blizzards, once winding up a mile off course from the bus station due to poor visibility. In many instances the bus never arrived, so I had to walk back home frostbitten in my face and on my legs. I was the only student from the village who attended high school. One other boy from outside Hirschfeld joined me at the bus stop. His father was our physician in a nearby village and dropped his son off at the bus station in a black Mercedes.

Due to poor nutrition and curriculum changes from one high school to another, my grades dropped tremendously. Previously an A-B student, I now was a C-D student. My parents decided to move me to a Realschule which was one level lower than the Gymnasium to prepare me for a mid level job instead of entering the university. This move didn't help me much either because the curriculum changes were drastic. Many courses were different from those in the high school. Once again, the tumbleweed lost the link to all of the major subjects.

Desperately trying to find the right solution, my parents moved me once more to a Handelsschule (Commercial School) to prepare me for entrance to a commercial pursuit. I still remained a C-student in that school but finally graduated after two years (U.S. high school equivalency).

Little did I know that this interest in commercial business world would play a key role in my later career in America when I became an International Trade Specialist for the United States. But there would be many years of tumbleweed turmoil before that would happen. Meanwhile, in Traben-Trarbach, my life revolved around school, and, oh yes, those vine-covered hills of the Mosel Valley.

These steep slopes found around the Mosel region are some of the most labor intensive vineyards in the world. Even today mechanical harvesting is impractical on these steep hills. When I turned 16 I was allowed to join the harvesting of the grapes during my fall vacation. It was a painstaking chore trying to keep my balance while plucking grapes from vines staked upright on the sloping hillsides. I'd pick small bundles of grapes and hand them over to men carrying large containers on their backs. They carried the grapes to the trucks. It was a dangerous job since the slopes were roughly equivalent to standing on the rooftop of a typical American home.

Because of my schooling outside the village, my daily transportation timetable, and working at grape harvesting, I remained an outcast among the village kids. We were refugees and not natives. I was the teacher's daughter who spoke High German at all times and not the Hunsrueck dialect the other kids spoke.   Even with my classmates in school I had no connection beyond the classroom. After school everybody went home to their own villages. After-school activities were not available.   To be active in sports or music one had to be a member of the Sport- or Musikverein (clubs).   For me that was not possible since I had to care for my brothers in the afternoons and had neither money nor transportation for such after school activities. I eventually found a good friend who was somewhat in the same boat as I was.   Her father had been a French soldier who had been killed in World War II.   The mother, who never got over that loss, suffered greatly from anxiety and was not well accepted by the Hirschfeld people. They considered her strange.   My friend's grandfather had a small farm and also was the administrator at the local Co-op.

During summer vacations my girlfriend and I were inseparable. My mother wasn't teaching her home economics class and was therefore home with my brothers in the afternoons. This gave me considerable time to spend with my friend. I helped her milk their cows in the evenings while her family was still in the fields. We cleaned the stalls and piled the cow dung onto the dung pile in front of their barn. It was hard work that normally men would perform.   As a reward I was able to eat dinner with them, food that I couldn't get at home.

Both 16, we were allowed to go to the local Gasthaus (Pub) on Saturday nights which was about one mile away from the village, near the train station. There we met other kids from Hirschfeld and surrounding villages. We listened to the jukebox, talked and had fun. Gertrud was allowed to stay until midnight and get a ride home with someone from the village, but I – teacher's daughter -- had to be home by 9:00 p.m. And that was just the time when the fun really began. My father didn't care how I got home as long as I was home by that time.

Lonely and scared I walked the mile in darkness waiting to get past the woods to finally see our house from the distance. I hid in the ditch along the street or behind a tree when I saw oncoming cars. Blinded by the lights and by my tears, I asked God to protect me on the way home and questioned him why I couldn't be a farmer's daughter. At home I rang the doorbell to be let in. This gave my father a chance to look at the clock. One minute late, and I could expect a punishment.

This all changed at the age of 17 when I met a boy who had a brand new white Volkswagen Beetle. Such a car was a rarity since most kids didn't have any transportation. He lived in Lautzenhausen, a village just outside the U.S. Hahn Air Base gate. He was a farm boy and a terrific dancer. He picked me up on Saturdays and took me to the local dances or to the NCO Club at the Air Base where large bands were playing Glen Miller songs, my favorite.

"You dance like a butterfly," he used to say.

We had such a good time. He didn't seem to mind bringing me home at 10:00 p.m., my new curfew time. We dated for about a year until one Saturday night when he didn't show up at my house. I was very concerned that maybe he had had a car accident because it wasn't like him not to show up without saying anything. Since my parents didn't have a telephone but his did, I called his house from our village post office. His grandmother answered but would not bring him to the phone or take a message. I was heartbroken. One day I took a bus to Lautzenhausen to see if I could meet with him. I caught him outside tending to his family's Misthaufen (dung pile).

"What happened? Why are you not coming anymore to pick me up for the dances?" I asked.

"My father won't allow it anymore. He'll take my car away from me if I see you again."

"What? Why?"

"One of the men from your village came to my father and told him that you were a whore who slept with everybody."

"Who is saying such things about me?" I cried,

"I know that this is not true," he told me. "You are a wonderful girl, and I like you very much, but my hands are tied. Besides you are a school teacher's daughter, and not a farm girl," he continued as he looked over his shoulder toward his house.

He was afraid that his father or his grandmother might see me talking to him. I started to get dizzy and almost fainted right in front of him. I couldn't believe what I had just heard. He told me the name of the man from Hirschfeld and went quickly inside his barn.

When I returned home I immediately told my mother about the meeting. She ran out of the house and down the street where the family lived to let them know that she didn't appreciate this type of slander. The confrontation got pretty heated. Mutti was furious when she returned home, and it took a while for her to calm down. The family had two girls a year older than I was. Since they didn't have any boyfriends with cars, they thought I shouldn't either. Such was the life of a refugee tumbleweed in a small, and small-minded, German farm village, so different from Wohnroth where the people had been warm and welcoming.

After graduating from the School of Commerce, I had not been able to find a job in the local area. My parents would soon be ready to move on once Vati completed his five years of teaching which he owed the State of Rheinland Pfalz.

Vati had been trying to resolve issues with the two Hirschfeld pastors. The division between Catholics and Protestants in the village was beginning to have an effect on us. It seemed one side or the other wanted support from Vati while he attempted to remain neutral. Given what seemed an impasse, Vati was ready to move to the Protestant state of Niedersachsen where he had heard teacher positions might be available. The winds of change were once again beginning to ruffle the tumbleweed's branches.

An American Air Base

There was, however, one source of employment near Hirschfeld that I thought might offer me an opportunity. That was the American air base I had visited at the NCO Club when dancing with my boyfriend. Since I had taken a couple years of English in school, I decided to apply, without the knowledge of my parents, for a clerk typist position in the Civilian Personnel Office. The base, known as Hahn Air Base, was an American airfield located about six miles from Hirschfeld.

My English was a two-year school English, not good enough to hold a lengthy conversation, but sufficient, I thought, for an office job where German civilian staff worked. I thought that if only Germans, except the American Director, worked in that office, I would not have much contact with the soldiers and my father would approve. It was likely that I would work there only for one year anyway since Vati had received approval for his assignment to the State of Niedersachsen for the summer of 1964. At that time it was understood I would be going with the family.

I enjoyed my job on the base very much. It paid well in comparison to German office workers in the surrounding towns even though most of the money I earned I had to give to my parents for room and board. I earned DM80 a month (eighty marks, roughly twenty U.S. dollars). Of this, my father collected sixty marks. Being employed, he said, meant I had to pay my share of living expenses.

One of my duties as clerk was to walk up the street to the Headquarters Building and pick up mail and paperwork. Every Friday I stopped in at the Information Office and picked up a few copies of the weekly newspaper *Hahn Hawk*. It was an English language paper for the base's airmen, but it always had a page in German for the civilian employees. So, I'd pick up the paper and briefly talk to Frau Fink, the Community Relations advisor, who was a German national. She always had a joke in store for me.

It was in October, 1963, that she called over an airman from the office while I was talking to her. She said, "Tilty would like to speak with you, Josefine."

"Now? Who is Tilty?" I asked.

"Wes, the handsome airman who is our sports editor," she replied.

I had seen him before during my visits but ignored him. I thought he was sort of cute, in fact very handsome, but not for me. Tilty came over, Frau Fink introduced us, and right away he asked me if I wanted to join him for a Halloween party some of the airmen were planning.

"I don't know if I can. I have to ask my parents first," I said to him.

"Ok, let me know as soon as possible," he replied.

I didn't know it at the time, but following my previous visit to the office, "Tilty" had asked Frau Fink to introduce us on my next visit. For this introduction Frau Fink asked him for a pack of Pall Mall cigarettes. She had told him that German custom called for a payment in return for a formal introduction. That wasn't true. It was just another of Frau Fink's jokes. But Airman Tilton hustled over to the BX and bought her a pack of cigarettes. It cost him 13¢.

After work that day, the way I expressed it to my parents was, "I've been invited to a Halloween party and I must attend." Truth be told, neither my parents nor I really knew just what a Halloween party was. Halloween, with its trick-or-treat, garish costumes, and parties was not something we Germans were familiar with. Germans do have similar traditions on a holiday we call Fasching, best known to Americans as "Mardi Gras" especially in New Orleans. But there stood the tumbleweed trying to bulldoze her way to gaining parental approval. I should have been able to predict my father's response.

"Is he an American soldier?" Vati asked.

"Yes, he works at the Headquarters building," I replied.

"You know that I don't approve of these American soldiers. They are no good. Like soldiers everywhere. They get drunk and take advantage of the girls."

"He's not a soldier, Vati, he's an airman," I shot back. "It's the Air Force, like the German Luftwaffe." I thought an appeal to a well-known German class distinction might help.

"My reputation is at stake," he continued, again referring to his position as village teacher.

After a long discussion, he finally gave in and said, "As long as you are at home at 11:00 p.m. We will let you go this time. But don't get any ideas about getting involved with an American. You know that we will be moving north next year, and you are coming with us."

On the 31st of October, the day of the party, I waited impatiently for Wes. He was late, and I thought he wasn't coming to pick me up. He arrived about an hour late in a borrowed car from his sergeant. He brought me a bottle of bubble bath. I had never seen bubble bath and was wondering if that was a hint that I smelled bad. He had been in Trier all day typesetting and writing headlines for the *Hahn Hawk* newspaper, and on the way home he had witnessed a fatal car accident which made him late. He had rendered help to one victim and had seen a decapitated driver in another car. He had to wait at the scene for a long time because the German police needed an interpreter to take his statement. It had been a long day for Wes. He hadn't eaten anything. And then, at the last minute, he told me of a change in plans.

"The Halloween party has been canceled, Josefine, but I would like to take you out to dinner instead. We could go to Bernkastel on the Mosel River," he said.

I wasn't about to divulge this to Vati, so I hopped into his borrowed car.

He didn't know that I already had eaten at home since he was late to arrive and Vati had told me not to accept anything from a man. I was to order only what I could pay for myself.

In the Bernkastel restaurant, Wes ordered a Rumpsteak with Pommes, and I ordered a glass of wine. He was puzzled why I had no appetite, but I explained it away and we had a wonderful time. Wes talked about his home state, California, and I, in my broken English, about my family. A German-English dictionary was my steady companion. Punctually at 11:00 p.m. I was back home ringing the door bell for my parents to open the door. Wes gave me a little kiss on my cheek and returned back to his barracks.

The next day Mutti and I left for a two-week trip we had planned to see her Uncle Hans in Schnackenburg, far to the north along the Elbe River. On the train, I told Mutti about my date with Wes.

"He will be my husband some day, I know," I said to Mutti who was trying to interest me in a German soldier who was standing near the window in front of our train compartment.

"Are you out of your mind?" she replied. "Haven't you heard enough about these soldiers from the base? They take German girls to the U.S. only for them to find out that their 'Americans' were living in shacks, somewhere in the hills." It was a well-worn story.

"Mutti, he's not from the hills. He's from California," I said with a tone that implied I knew something about that state.

"Vati will never allow you to marry an American soldier. Get this out of your head," she nervously replied. And there the topic rested. For a few days.

While at Uncle Hans' I received a letter from Wes every other day telling me how much he missed me and about his trip to Berlin while I was in Schnackenburg. He was covering a sports story in Berlin and was traveling with the base's basketball team. The tournament in Berlin was on November 22, 1963. That was the day President Kennedy was shot in Dallas, Texas. Kennedy was very popular among Germans, and especially those in Berlin. To this day I don't know whether the outpouring of German sympathy played a role in softening my father's attitude toward American "soldiers," but for days after that tragic event Wes was still in Berlin. His trip back to Hahn Air Base had been postponed due to the incident and the high alert the American bases in Germany were under.

The world was shocked, and especially so were the Berliners. They had been very fond of President Kennedy since his speech in their city the previous June. "Ich bin ein Berliner" had warmed their hearts and given them hope in the shadow of that wall dividing their city. The wall had made it even more difficult for East Germans to escape. Gone were the simple barbed wire barriers my family negotiated in our own escape. Kennedy's death had a huge impact on the city of Berlin.

Wes observed the outpouring of grief and sympathy in the city and wrote an article "Berlin 'City of Grief' after President's Death." Excerpts of the article were sent worldwide over the UP/AP wire system. While Mutti and I were following events from my great uncle's home in Schnackenburg, Wes wrote, *"I had the opportunity to take a tour of the Western portion of this city, and came to a spot near that despicable wall where only a few months ago Kennedy had spoken. I noticed a small wooden cross, apparently recently made, planted near the memorial of Peter Fechter, a 17-old youth who bled to death at that spot after being shot in an escape attempt. At the foot of this simple monument was a wreath of flowers, and on a plaque the words, "John F. Kennedy, 'Ich bin ein Berliner'" were printed. It became most obvious to me that he had owned the hearts of these people. Every West German flag was flown at half-mast that Saturday as most flags around the world were, and on those so affixed that they could not be lowered, a black banner was attached. Again I thought, "He certainly held the hope and respect of these people."......*

Back at work at Hahn Air Base, Wes picked me up every morning at the bus stop outside the base gate and walked me to my office. At lunch he took me to the Airmen's' Club. It was like we were meant to be together. One day in December 1963, during lunch at a Gasthaus in Lautzenhausen, outside the base gate, he asked me to marry him. It wasn't a fancy proposal. He didn't fall on his knees or have it announced by an airplane pulling a banner. He just opened a small box and gave me a simple 14k gold ring which he had bought for $13 in the BX. Thirteen dollars was a third of his two-week paycheck. I don't even remember him asking me with the words, "Will you marry me?" We both seemed to simply understand that that was what we were destined to do.

"I'll need your birth certificate, your parent's signature, and some other paperwork so I can request the Base Commander's official approval," he said. He had already been checking the Air Force regulations.

"We also have to go to the Base Chaplain to see if he will marry us since you are Lutheran and I am Catholic," he said. "This process will take about three months when a German national is involved," he continued.

We briefly talked about a date of the wedding and decided we'd get married in October 1964 after he turned 21 so that he wouldn't have to have any signature from his parents. After that we both went back to work.

On the way home from work I hid the ring from my parents because Wes had not asked my father yet for his blessings. I stayed in cloud nine for a few days until I decided to let my mother know that Wes would ask Vati for his blessings on my 18th birthday which was December 27th.

"Isn't this a bit early? You've known each other for only three months," she said.

"I know. But I also know that he is the right man," I replied.

She didn't say any more. She knew that the big task was to bring the news to Vati and she wasn't certain how he might react to it.

Wes received his acceptance by the rest of my family, especially my brothers, through their stomachs. After Thanksgiving he brought a 20 lb turkey from the commissary. This he baked in our oven. Somehow, despite his limited German, he managed to arrange with Mutti that he would bring a turkey, and cook it, if she would prepare the side dishes. It turned out Wes had had some cooking experience back in California while his mother was healing from a broken leg. Unaware of our food situation, he was amazed that not one ounce of meat was left on the turkey after the meal. Nothing but clean bones. It was a real treat for all of us. The last time we had eaten turkey was at Mama's in East Germany.

Even Mama was at our house during that Thanksgiving meal. Papa had died just months before I met Wes. Mama and Papa had escaped to West Germany on August 12, 1961, the day before East Germany had been completely cut off to the West by the Berlin Wall.

From that time on, the 104 mile-long wall surrounding Berlin replaced the old barbed wire fences and wooden checkpoint stations. The new barrier in Berlin included guard towers placed along large concrete walls which surrounded a wide area, later known as the "death strip" because it contained anti-vehicle trenches, land mines, machine-gun posts, and other defenses. The Soviet-dominated Eastern Bloc officially claimed that the wall was erected to protect its population from "fascist elements" conspiring to prevent the "will of the people" in building a Socialist State in East Germany. They neglected to mention that in practice the wall served to prevent people like my own family from making a defection, as we had done, from Germany's communist Eastern Bloc.

I am quite sure that my grandparents knew of the newly erected wall in Berlin and the tighter closure to the West. Mama's ears must have been pressed daily to her little radio. They had been harassed by the officials since our escape and could not longer tolerate this harassment. They left their house and belongings to their youngest son and came directly to us in Hirschfeld without having to stay at the refugee camp. After all, being "senior citizens" they were – unofficially, of course – welcome to "escape" to the West. Still, the stress they endured took a toll on Papa. He died of a sudden heart attack after only two years of living in Hirschfeld.

Even after that great turkey dinner, however, Vati still had to be a little more convinced about the idea of me dating an American soldier. Whenever possible, on Sunday afternoon visits, Wes and Vati played a game of chess, even though they couldn't communicate verbally. Vati didn't speak any English and Wes very little German. But Wes knew that chess was another form of communication.

Finally, the day arrived for Wes to ask Vati's blessings for our engagement. It was my 18th birthday. I wrote a couple of German sentences on a piece of paper and taught Wes how to pronounce them. Wes and I sat with my parents in the living room when Wes started to read the note in his broken German. "Ich moechte Sie etwas fragen, Mr. Lohse," he said.

But Vati interrupted him immediately when he saw how Wes struggled to get the words out and said, "I know what you want to ask. Mutti already informed me about this."

Mutti didn't wait to let him finish. Besides, Wes had not understood a single word Vati had spoken. She reached for a bottle of champagne she had hidden behind the couch. She then threw a crystal wine glass against the wall. Wes shaken by this action asked me what was happening. "Are your parents angry?"

"No. The opposite. This is for good luck. It is a German custom," I said.

He didn't seem too convinced about this sort of custom. He looked ready to bolt for the door and leave this "nut house." We all started laughing. Vati gave his blessings, we all drank champagne, and the tumbleweed was officially engaged to an American airman.

My life's struggles, however, were anything but over. Even with the hardships of the post war years with Russian soldiers controlling our lives, then the Communist interference in every aspect of my parents lives, our harrowing escape to the West, the refugee camp in Berlin, the "scrape-it-together years in Wohnroth, the foster home in Worms, and the lack of being accepted in Hirschfeld, more of my life's struggles lay yet before me than behind me. And these would begin just down the street in our backwards little farming village.

Some of the villagers did not like that I as a school teacher's daughter had been working at a U.S. military base and was engaged to an American soldier. They actually didn't like us at all. In their eyes we had invaded their village as refugees and didn't fit into their farm community. According to them, dating an American soldier wasn't the right example to set. Some of them called me a whore while walking down the street. Others said that I had been "stung by a bee" since they thought, erroneously, that I was pregnant and had to get married.

Wes rented a room in Hirschfeld at my girlfriend's house across from the Backhaus. Not owning a car, we both rode the bus to and from work, and after we both came home in the evenings, I spent time at his place to fix him dinner. The legal curfew for unmarried couples was 10:00 p.m. On the way home I would occasionally see neighbors moving curtains to see if I went home on time.

My parents were scheduled to move in June of 1964 to the State of Niedersachsen. Although I was now engaged, Vati insisted that I move with them since I was not yet 21 and had no place to live. Apartments were not available in the area. He secretly thought the distance and new surroundings might influence me to forget about Wes. Apparently, his blessings didn't mean as much to him as they had to me, I thought.

In order to fix this dilemma, Wes and I decided to get married in April before their move. Wes requested right away the signature and approval from his parents in California. This would allow us to get married before October. But he did not receive a response. His parents, we later learned, were not in favor of him marrying a German girl. His parents still remembered WWII and didn't like Germans. The lack of response surprised Wes.

"No one on either side of our family fought in the war in Europe," he told me. "I would not expect any resistance based on you being German. It's probably because my two older brothers aren't yet married, so my parents see me as too young."

Whatever their reason for silence, it didn't bode well for the tumbleweed.

"I am sorry but I won't give you a signature either," Vati said to me after we gave him the news. Wes and I were devastated. We were running out of time. My father had made it clear he would not leave me behind.

Wes immediately sent off a telegram to his parents requesting their signature stating, "Problems arising. Need signature ASAP." He left the rest to their imagination.

Married to an American

Within one week the signatures arrived, and so we scheduled the wedding for April 4th in the Base Chapel at Hahn Air Base. Of course, we had to have the German civil ceremony as well, and that we did April 3rd in the town nearest the base. Our wedding was a very small affair of about 20 people. We had no relatives in the area, and Wes' were in the States. We borrowed Wes' sergeant's car to get to church. My parents arranged for a small dinner at the house. Wes bought me the wedding dress from a small shop in Traben-Trarbach. It was a light blue suit of good quality which I could wear on other occasions. My wedding bouquet consisted of 18 red carnations, the number of my age.

After the wedding, the tumbleweed was once again in motion, however short the journey. I moved in with Wes in his one-room apartment in a brand new farm house belonging to my girlfriend's family. We divided the room up in thirds with fabric hanging from the ceiling. This set up provided us living, sleeping, and eating areas. We had an oil burning stove which had a hot plate for one pot. That was our kitchen. We bought 5-gallon containers of heating oil each payday on the base, and carried it on the bus to Hirschfeld. That was our fuel for heating and cooking. We shared the second floor bathroom with the farm family which had become our landlord. They allowed us, which was their own practice, to bathe only on Saturdays. There was a hot water tank mounted on the wall above the foot of the tub. Wes' first experience with this had taught him firsthand the realities of life in a small German farm village. It happened his first Saturday in the "room" which we called an "apartment." I was still living up the street with my parents at the time. He had donned a robe and headed for the bathroom.

"I studied the plumbing set-up for a while," he told me, "and found only one faucet, and that was attached to the wall-mounted tank. So, I tried that. It was ice-cold. So I looked for a switch or a thermostat. Checked every wall in the bathroom. No luck." I tried to squelch a smile I felt creeping up on me, though, in truth, I didn't know how the landlord's tub worked either. Ours in our school house apartment had a switch right on the side of the water heater. It was electric. So I waited as Wes' story went on.

"Well then I noticed a small metal door down low on the side of the water heater. I expected to find a switch. Guess what I found?"

I really didn't know what he might have found. So I shrugged.

"Nothing," Wes said. "Nothing but a handful of ashes!"

Wes had learned the hard way. The water tank had to be heated by burning coal before taking a bath. He had gone to the landlord who was out in the barn and used his very limited

German language to explain his plight. The farmer had given Wes a bucket and pointed to a pile of coal. This procedure took about an hour, and then there'd be only enough hot water for one tub full. Which meant that after I moved in, Wes and I would have to share the hot water. Ah, life was tough!

In June my parents moved to the State of Niedersachsen to a village near Hannover called Ohrdorf. This was about three miles from the barbed-wire border between East and West Germany. Odd that having escaped from the communist east, they again lived so close to the dreaded regime. But Ohrdorf was a peaceful place, a village of considerably more substance than Hirschfeld had been. The farmers owned a lot more land, and most of them had large estates. My father was not a refugee there. He was an experienced teacher from another state who had transferred to fill an open position.

I continued working on the air base until the fall when I became pregnant with our first child. The one room was getting too small so we moved to a brand new apartment directly above the village store. The rooms were located along a long hallway similar to a hotel floor. The hallway wasn't finished. The grey block stones were still visible. There was no plaster or paint on the walls. One room was the kitchen, one the bedroom, one the living room and one the bathroom. The rooms were fairly large with windows overlooking the village square. While Wes was at work I stayed in the apartment and did needlepoint pictures for the baby and pillow cases for our living room couch. One morning when I was in the store below, I overheard a conversation between two women.

"Did you hear about that Finche (that is what they called me instead of Josefine)?" one asked the other.

"They say they saw her dancing naked on the table in front of their window," she laughed.

I stood at the freezer compartment behind a couple of shelves and almost fainted. I left my grocery basket on the floor and stepped through the backdoor and ran up to my apartment. I wanted to share this slandering news with my parents and with Wes but couldn't. We had no telephone. Instead I cried the entire afternoon until Wes came home from work unable to comprehend such awful talk which was spreading through the village like wild fire. I began to understand why my parents decided to move away from Hirschfeld. It was pretty clear by now. These people continued to show a mean spirit and their ignorance. Right before the baby was born we moved once more to a larger village located only two miles from Hahn Air Base. No one knew us there which gave us peace and quiet. The apartment was located in the farmers Co-op. The Co-op manager and his family lived across the hall from us. He gave us a small piece of ground behind the building for gardening. The villagers who walked by were astonished to see that the

American could grow a garden like the Germans. All rows were straight and orderly, and no weeds between the vegetables.

Our daughter Iris was born in May 1965. She was a beautiful baby, and Wes and I were extremely happy. Mutti came to visit to help me out the first couple of weeks since Iris was very colicky and cried throughout the night not giving me much sleep. Now, especially with the baby, we needed desperately to get to and back from the base so Wes bought a used Nash Rambler. While he attended a 12-week college course in Frankfurt to learn German which ultimately started a 23 year college night school career, I took my driver's license on base. I walked into the Transportation Squadron, took a written test and a guy took me around the block for a driving test, and so I drove home. That was it. No driving school. A week later I drove the car to see my grandmother in Neuburg near Karlsruhe, about a two hour-drive.

Wes' orders to return to the U.S. came in January 1966. He received an assignment to Niagara Falls Air Station, in the State of New York. The news was exciting for us but I began to wonder if I had done the right thing. My parents were devastated to have their only daughter move so far away. I was no less unsettled than they. My tumbleweed bones were all aquiver at the prospect of leaving my family, my homeland, even my language. It was one thing to marry an American and continue living in Germany as we had been doing for almost two years. It occurred to me that I could walk, if necessary, from the American base at Hahn to where my parents then lived in north Germany. But walk? From America?

The day before our departure, I went to the base and waited for Wes in the recreation center. He was still at work. I attended to Iris in the baby stroller when a former boyfriend tapped me on my back.

"Hello Finche," he greeted me. "What are you doing here?" It was the fellow from Hirschfeld whose family would not allow him to date me. His family was Catholic. I was Lutheran.

"I am waiting for Wes. We are leaving for the U.S. tomorrow," I replied.

We both sat on the bench. His eyes filled with tears. He looked at Iris in the stroller and said, "This could have been my baby. But you know that my grandmother and your parents did not want us to date. You being Lutheran, and I am Catholic, besides I was five years older."

"I know," I said.

We spoke of the journey before me. It seemed unfathomable to both of us. So far beyond that highway we knew as the Hunsrueck Hoehenstrasse, our only connection from a quaint, backwards little village to the outside world.

"I wish you the best, Finche. Good Bye," he replied and left.

He had secretly been my first big love, despite our parents' objections. I was crazy about him. It was more of a puppy love than anything else. However, every place Wes and I lived after we were married I had noticed him. He'd be visiting someone across the street hoping to see me walk out of the apartment. We never met, though, after my wedding. This chance meeting on the air base was really not something I wanted to happen just before my departure to the big foreign country. I had no idea that he cared about me that much. I thought about him often after that. Today he and his family communicate with me at least twice a year. He calls me on my birthday and I call him on his.

The next day, Wes and I met my parents and brothers at Rhein Main Air Base, just across the runway from the civilian airport in Frankfurt. It was one of my saddest and happiest days of my life. There it was again. That hungry-but-not-hungry feeling. My mother tried very hard to hold away her tears. My brothers didn't speak at all. It was as if they were in shock. Even Vati was very quiet. He took a last minute picture of Wes, me and Iris and then my parents left. A new adventure was about to begin for me, as were a host of new challenges. This time the tumbleweed wouldn't snag a rusty fence until it had blown some 4,000 miles.

A New Homeland

A new immigrant was about to enter the U.S. at McGuire Air Force Base in the state of New Jersey. As we landed at the base I began to cry. I was a jumble of joy, fear, and homesickness. It's worth noting that at this point in my life I still did not know that I was a tumbleweed. In fact, I had never seen much less heard about a tumbleweed. But that would soon change. Maybe this would be a good point to share what little I know even today about this little plant. No need for in-depth research here. This is not a botanist's doctoral dissertation. My own memory plus a little input from Wikipedia will suffice. Though most Americans today have seen tumbleweeds, or at least seen pictures of them in Hollywood's western movie productions, most probably think tumbleweeds date back to the time of pre-white-man Indians. Well, America's early Indians might have seen windblown dried, even rounded, weeds, but they did not see tumbleweeds here any more than I did in my village of Kleinforst. No, the tumbleweed – just as I am – is an immigrant to this country. And, like me, a European immigrant. In fact, it's a post-Civil War immigrant. Wikipedia puts it this way, "It seems to have been imported into South Dakota from Russia in 1870 or 1874 in shipments of flaxseed." The plant we know as a North American desert tumbleweed is actually a Russian thistle known as "*Salsola tragus*, an annual plant that disengages from its root, actually breaking off at its stem base." It then tumbles away in the wind. It has become an itinerant that "disperses its seeds as it rolls on top of the ground."

Now, although I do have four grandchildren, I may not actually claim that I was "spreading seeds," but like the tumbleweed, I have often disengaged from my roots, tumbled away in the winds of change, and snagged somewhere to begin life anew. So it's not a stretch of the imagination that I've come to be known by family and friends as a tumbleweed. That said, we can return to the most dramatic uprooting of my life and my first coast to coast American journey where I did, in fact, see my first tumbleweed.

I was not yet 21-years-old when I stepped down from the airplane in New Jersey. I was about to start life anew as a wife, a mother, and a stranger in a "foreign country." I was in an unfamiliar environment; the only people I knew were my husband and my infant daughter. I was not yet fluent in the English language. I had married a man I had known only a little more than two years and as I was stepping down from the airplane, I realized had no idea where he came from. Sure, I knew he was from California, but I knew literally nothing about life in California. I had not seen any of his family or friends. Suddenly I began to remember the horror stories about German girls who came to the U.S. only to find out that their husbands were liars. Was I about to become one of those? Wes had been good to me since we were married, and I had no doubts that he was a true man. But, oh, the uncertainty of it all!

After spending the night at McGuire we headed for the Bayonne harbor in New York City. Here we would pick up our Rambler which Wes had shipped a few weeks earlier from northern Germany. The New York subway was an eye opener for me. People didn't seem very friendly. Everyone was in such a hurry. In response to our questions on the subway we most often received no answers. The hustle and bustle trying to reach the harbor was extremely stressful, especially since I was trying to negotiate the subways with our infant daughter in a stroller. We did manage to find the port at Bayonne and even our car. The traffic out of the harbor area was an overwhelming onslaught of motion, noise, and chaos. I had never seen so many cars on the road and so many highway lanes and bridges and tunnels. Not only that, but we were frantically searching for two things – a filling station since the car was shipped with only three gallons of gasoline, and a place to buy auto insurance.

Instead of heading directly to our assignment in Niagara Falls, we had decided we would drive to California and see Wes' parents. Although they hadn't approved of our marriage, Wes wanted to show them that I was a decent girl, and of course he wanted to show off his daughter, Iris, now just short of a year-old.

Our first stop was in Dayton, Ohio, to visit Wes' aunt. On our third day in the U.S. on the way to visit a friend who had attended our wedding at Hahn Air Base, we were approaching Columbus, Ohio, when the shock and challenges of my "new land" began in earnest. We were shot at by occupants of an oncoming car! As we approached, the driver held a pistol out of his window and shot. We had all windows open in our car. I had just put Iris down in the back seat and got settled in front again when this happened. We could hear the shot but were not clear whether the bullet flew through the open back windows or across the hood and into the surrounding corn fields. In shock we stopped at the nearest police station and reported the incident but couldn't adequately identify the car or the driver. It had all happened too fast. It was a time of riots and racial unrest in the U.S., but Wes had seen three occupants in a two-tone green car. All were white. The driver, with blond hair, had a pistol in his left hand, and fired. More than that we could not tell the police.

"I want to go back home," I told Wes. "I am afraid here in the U.S. This is like the Wild West I have heard about. People shooting," I cried.

We still had some 6,000 miles to drive to and from California before we'd reach our new home in Niagara Falls. I found myself checking every oncoming car to see if someone held a pistol out of the window. We followed Highway 66 from St. Louis through the deserts of New Mexico and Arizona into California. The scenery was breathtaking and exciting. I had never seen a desert before. And, yes, somewhere along that route I saw my first tumbleweed.

There was not much traffic on the wide straight highways. Sometimes I was a little afraid that if we had car troubles with our old Rambler, no one would come by and assist us. The signs "Last Gas Station" made me wonder if we would make it out of the desert and into California. The clear blue sky every day was a phenomenon I wasn't used to at all. That, and the people we met out in the West, began to put me at ease. They seemed friendly and genuine. The desert and its people, however, were a much warmer welcome than what I was soon to receive from Wes' mother.

We arrived in California after six days' driving from one American coast to the other – and this was before the time of today's web of multi-lane Interstate highways. For a young German girl who had never been outside a country about the size of Oregon, it was an unimaginable journey! And Wes' mother? She made no effort to welcome or accept me at all. She ignored me while I was there and took her sister out shopping, and went to a hairdresser, leaving me behind. I would have dearly enjoyed seeing the American stores, and after that daunting cross-country trip, going to the hairdresser would also have been a welcome event. The first of my huge challenges in adapting to a new land and a new culture had just slapped me in the face. I don't know which was more of a shock, the bullet-shot in Ohio, or Wes' mother. We didn't do much sightseeing while in California, and began our return trip to Niagara Falls after only three-day's stay.

On the way east we drove through Dayton, Ohio, to pick up some things from Wes' aunt, who, incidentally, took me shopping and to a hairdresser. She and Wes' Uncle Mac had been in Europe during their Air Force career, and were much more welcoming than her sister in California.

Niagara Falls was a good assignment for Wes. He was back in the U.S., and the job seemed to go well. A Staff Sergeant at that time didn't earn very much money, and with our first move as with others to follow, we had to make our first trip to a credit agency to get credit for apartment, telephone and utility deposits. In order to make ends meet and have a new car we desperately needed, Wes took a weekend job in a gas station, working Friday and Saturday nights. During the week he went to work at his Air Force job at the Air Station. Two nights in the evenings he attended college classes at a local college. His goal was to eventually become an officer.

The tumbleweed remained in motion even within Niagara Falls. We moved from a too-small apartment to a too-old house before we finally were able to get an apartment in military housing. I applied in town for a job as a waitress, but was turned down. My English wasn't good enough. That only made me more determined to keep trying. Barriers, frustrations, and denials would continue to plague me in my search for employment for years to come.

Our son Eric was born in Niagara Falls in 1967. My parents flew from Germany and visited us that summer. They were anxious to find out where their daughter had settled and how she was faring in America.

Our next assignment, in 1968, was to San Bernardino, California. Again, we drove across the U.S. on Route 66 which had become my favorite route. I had come to love the desert, the openness, the wide roads and the truckers who helped us navigate. Traveling now with two children, we developed a daily routine. We started driving early in the morning around 4:30 a.m.. The kids were still sleeping in the back of the car. Around 7:30 a.m. we'd stop for breakfast and then keep driving until lunchtime. For lunch we'd stop in some little town and find a park where we'd eat sandwiches while the kids could run around a bit. Our final stop would be around 3:30 p.m. The small motels we could afford usually didn't have a pool. So, we turned on the water in the bath tub and let the kids play which gave us a few minutes to unwind. We had our trips down to a science.

In San Bernardino times were hard for us financially. I applied for several different jobs but was always turned down due to the fact that I didn't have any U.S. experience or because I was a military spouse.

"Your husband could be transferred at any time," was the line I heard each time I applied for a job.

I was getting frustrated. I was willing to work and learn but no one would give me a chance. It seemed that the Americans didn't like their military families. I felt like we were just a nuisance. The Vietnam War was still going strong. At the employment office I visited one day I was told again that they didn't have anything for me because I didn't have any American experience and was not a citizen. Frustrated and angry I sarcastically asked the lady at the desk, "Does a prostitute have to have experience in your country?" She looked bewildered. No one had ever asked her a question like that. I had no intention of entering the world's oldest female profession. I simply wanted to make a point.

After several months, I finally got my first job in America, waitressing in a cafeteria-style restaurant. How did I know that most waitresses would accept a job in that kind of restaurant because it was mostly self-service and tips were low?

In 1969, while we were still in San Bernardino, Wes applied for the military bootstrap program. He was accepted and was allowed time off with pay to finish his undergraduate studies. That was the good news. The downside was that he'd have to travel to Nebraska to attend the University of Omaha. He had 48 semester hours to finish in one year.

I decided to pack up the kids and go stay with my parents in Germany for that year. The plan was good, but it didn't last very long. After three months I was homesick for Wes and wanted to rejoin him in Omaha. So I packed up again and flew back to the U.S. to Omaha. We rented a small furnished house. It was by no means a model home but it served its purpose. I knew it would only be for nine months. Wes went to school during the day, and I waitressed at night having finally been accepted as an "experienced" applicant.

His graduation day from the University of Nebraska at Omaha was one of our happiest, but like a rose, it also had its thorns. Wes had followed his dream and finished his undergraduate studies. He was the only son who finished higher education, an accomplishment that only his grandfather had enjoyed. His father travelled from California to attend the graduation while his mother stayed home.

I liked his father very much. He was a kind man but had been prevented by his wife over the years to have any kind of relationship with his son and his children. To his mother, I would never be anything other than a German refugee, an outsider. Still, graduation day was momentous. It also meant that the tumbleweed would once again ride the wind.

With a degree in hand, Wes was ready to apply for a commission. A dream we both had. Our sacrifices were about to be paid off. So, again we packed up, left Omaha, and returned to San Bernardino where he had actually been assigned all the time he had been in college. He was accepted at the Officer Training School in San Antonio, Texas, where he completed his three-month training and became an Air Force officer. The training was pretty difficult for him emotionally. He was already a 27-year old TSgt with a lot of military experience but had to take orders from young upper OTS class college graduates. He called me on several occasions ready to quit the training. I begged him not to give up, that he had only a couple of weeks left and reassured him that he was no quitter and would not quit this time either. I flew to San Antonio for the graduation and was awed by the ceremony. After the commissioning, the new lieutenants threw their hats up in the air, and everybody had to pay the drill sergeant a dollar. What a wonderful day it was.

After the graduation, Wes received his first assignment as a lieutenant. The tumbleweed once again was at the mercy of winds of change. This time we'd follow America's highways to Malmstrom AFB in Great Falls, Montana. But not before our fourth trip along Highway 66, which led not to Montana, but to Indianapolis where we would live for three months while Wes would train as an Air Force public affairs officer. I stayed home with the kids. At Thanksgiving Wes invited to our dinner two Vietnamese officers who attended the same school. I was panic stricken. We lived in a scarcely furnished apartment and had virtually no dishes because all of our belongings were in transit. We ate from frozen dinner trays which I had washed and reused over and over again. It turned out to be a delightful afternoon. The Vietnamese were very gracious and interested in our traditional holiday. They enjoyed eating a turkey and didn't mind eating from reused frozen dinner trays. Their curiosity was heightened by the wishbone I had saved. I explained to them that someone who received the larger end after breaking it in two had to make a wish. We lost contact with these officers and don't know to this day whether they survived the war.

We left Indiana and moved to Montana in the middle of winter. Along the way, the fuel pump in our car broke down just as we crossed the border from Wyoming into Montana. We literally rolled without power downhill for over a mile and came to a stop in the parking lot of a rustic-looking motel. In today's world we would call it a flea bag. We found an Indian who informed us that the fuel pump needed to be removed. It was minus 20 F.

"Where do we get a new fuel pump in this cold weather?" Wes asked.

The Indian answered: "We don't have any on hand here. We need to have a new one shipped via a Greyhound bus from Sheridan, Wyoming."

Two days later, the fuel pump arrived on time, and the Indian replaced it with the old one. Not an easy task in that cold weather. We were very grateful to have found such a kind helpful person.

The unplanned additional day on the road –like this winter delay -- was an extra expense for us. The Air Force would reimburse us only the mileage to the next base and only so many overnights were allowed. So, once again, the cost of "duty travel" would take cash out of our pockets when we could least afford it.

We drove through wonderful Montana terrain on Hwy 87 through Billings and other smaller cities. As we came closer to Great Falls we were surprised how flat the area was. The Rocky Mountains were visible in the far western distance. We forgot that Montana was located at the Missouri River and near five waterfalls. We remembered pictures of Montana showing the snow caps of the Glacier State Park Mountains and the open terrain with wild horses. We learned later that Montana was a large wheat growing state.

We finally arrived at Malmstrom AFB, a small USAF Base but found out that there were no housing units available for us, and so we were off house hunting off base. Malmstrom's main mission was to maintain and operate the powerful Minuteman II missiles, and is, therefore, a very important base for the US Air Force. Wes was assigned as the Public Affairs Officer for the 24th Air Division, a part of North American Air Defense Command.

The cost of living in Montana was high, and as I had done in Omaha, I found work as a waitress to help make ends meet. Both my English and my experience level had improved, and this time being a military spouse did not become an issue. At that time we were living on base in a small carport housing unit. The restaurant was an upscale supper club. I worked during the evenings when Wes was home with the kids. Once or twice a week I had to work the lunch. It would be many months before I learned there would be other kinds of challenges I, as a foreigner in an American work environment, would have to face.

We enjoyed the State of Montana very much. During the summer we went fishing or hiking in the mountains. The wide open spaces made the skies seem endless. We often took a trip through Glacier Park. The towering mountains with the exquisite wildflowers and diverse wildlife reminded me much of the Alps. The winters in Montana were harsh. At times it went down to -44°F. It was so cold that our battery in the car one day split in half while the car was parked in the garage. But the weather was not all that was cold. Equally cold, in what would be a continuing theme in this tumbleweed's life, was my reception by some Americans.

One morning, for example, I attended an officers' wives tea when the conversation focused on the weather. The outside temperature was −40°F .

"The Chinook will arrive at 11:00 a.m. I heard on the news," one of the women said.

"We won't have to shovel snow anymore," another lady responded.

"What is a Chinook?" I asked. For me, it was a new English word. I had no idea what would be arriving at 11.

"These are warm coastal winds that come over the mountains," the first woman replied. "They come roaring in like a freight train, and when they arrive ... well, you'll soon see."

It was hard for me to believe that such a thing could be so exactly predicted. Sure enough the wind started to blow just after 10:30 a.m. and by 11 the temperature was rapidly rising. By the time I left that tea party around noon, the temperature had gone from −40°F to +30°F. But the chill inside the room I will remember just as long as I recall my first Chinook.

As a lieutenant's wife I had been given a booklet on etiquette for an Air Force officer's wife. I had studied the booklet and had decided I would attend the wives' teas and luncheons to support my husband in his career. During the "tea" the day of the Chinook, one of the ladies at the table asked me if I would be interested in attending another function at noon the following week. I explained to her that I would be working the lunch schedule that day at the supper club and couldn't make it.

She gave me a sharp look of disapproval, and quickly said, "I'd like you to visit me for lunch tomorrow. Noon. At my house."

It was clearly not an invitation. It was a command. A very chilly sounding command. And then she abruptly turned away from me and ignored me throughout the "tea."

The next day, I did as she asked, though I knew her remark was neither a question nor a social invitation. As I entered her hallway, and even before she asked me to come in, she said, "The reason I asked you to come today is that I must let you know what an unrespectable job you have. As an officer's wife, such work is unsuitable."

I almost fainted. "What is a respectable job?" I asked.

She replied, "Well, you know, a teacher or a nurse, or at least some sort of volunteer work."

"I am not ashamed to be a waitress," I told her, still standing just inside the door. "I would clean toilets if I had to in order to help out and feed my kids," I replied and stormed out of her house.

That was the last connection I have ever had with the wives club. But it was certainly not the final "cultural challenge" I would face in Montana. That took place at the restaurant.

I suppose we could quibble here whether the issue here is my "German" work ethic, or just my personal work ethic. In the end it makes no difference. I am German. I have a strong personal drive to achieve, to work "full tilt," to give an hour of work for an hour's pay. But as I learned in Montana, not every person shares this "give it your all" work ethic. Some people, in fact, seem to have quite the opposite view about work. Some would rather do as little as they can get away with and still collect a paycheck.

And – here comes the lesson of my Montana restaurant days – those who would rather not strive and "do the max" often feel threatened by those who work as I do. It was just this conflict which confronted me in the restaurant where I worked.

I hustled. I was given the "worst station" but somehow continued to earn the highest tips. I would not "hang around" waiting for something to do. If there was a lull in business, I'd shine and polish wine decanters, fill sugar bowls, wipe clean the salt and pepper dispensers, fold napkins, refill stocks of supplies, dust window ledges. In short, I would do anything that needed being done. But I would not sit around twiddling my thumbs or swap small-talk and gossip. And that led to my first encounter with a "back-stabber."

An envious head waitress, who happened also to be the manager's wife, reported that I had short-changed my bus-boy on tips, that I stood around at the bar smoking and gossiping, and that I refused to fill and clean salt, pepper, and sugar containers. Not an ounce of truth. But, nevertheless – and maybe just because he lacked the backbone to confront his wife – the manager called me in, told me what had been reported, and fired me on the spot.

I drove home in tears, got stopped by the state police for speeding (and later paid a $60 fine), and arrived home frustrated, hurt, and angry. Wes was away on a Temporary Duty Travel. I needed him so badly. If I just could talk to my mother, I thought. There was no way we could afford a three-minute phone call to Germany. Besides what could I say in three minutes anyway? My homesickness overwhelmed me once again.

Within a year we had our next assignment. The tumbleweed was about to be blown south. The next place I'd snag a fence would be in Colorado Springs, Colorado. Wes was assigned as a Public Affairs Officer for the Air Defense Headquarters. Although we liked Montana, we were happy to move south to a warmer climate. Compared to Montana it was.

In Colorado Springs we bought our first home. It was a brand new tri-level. From our family room window we could see the Rockies with Pikes Peak standing proud. Tired with waitressing and not being able to find any other employment, I decided to go to a local cosmetology school and learn that profession. My English was just barely good enough to understand the complicated theory portion of the course. Learning the other skills was no problem. I graduated at the top of the class and was elected as Miss Cosmetology. After a full year of studying, I took my State exam in Denver and passed it right away. I got my first job as a beautician, today called Hair Designer.

Things seemed to go pretty well until one day when Wes announced he had another assignment, this time to Thule, Greenland, but without his family. He had been promised an assignment to Germany if he would take this isolated posting.

We sold our house and moved into an apartment before Wes departed for Greenland. He had 30 days leave in order to get us all situated, and he used that time to teach Iris and Eric to swim. The apartment had a pool, and since I had never learned to swim, I was afraid of what might happen if one of the kids fell in. Before he left for Greenland, both kids could swim the length of the pool even when unexpectedly pushed or thrown in.

It was heart breaking to think that I had to be alone for a whole year. No family, no friends. I kept my job as a hair dresser to stay busy which made the separation easier to tolerate. I usually was home by the time the kids came home from school. It was quite a challenge for me, alone in this foreign country and having to do all the things that Wes normally would have done, such as paying bills or registering the car.

I'll never forget one of the experiences I encountered while he was away that year. Wes called me every weekend from Thule to let me know that he was okay and to make sure we were the same. In 1974 we didn't have a computer or a smart phone for texting or calling. To make the calls was pretty complicated. Wes had to make an appointment with the telephone operator for a particular time at Goose Bay in Labrador, Canada, so she could connect us with the U.S. It was nearly impossible for me to call him from the U.S.

On one such call he talked to me about our two Dachshunds.

"Call the vet and get some shots for the dogs," Wes said one day as he phoned from his base in Greenland.

"Easier said than done," I thought to myself. What is a vet? I looked in the phone book under "Vet" and found Veterans Administration. At the time I didn't know how the word Veterinarian was spelled. I also didn't know what the

Veterans Administration was. So I called the VA and spoke to a lady on the phone.

"I would like to schedule my dogs for their shots," I said. She smiled at the other end. I could feel it right through the phone line. But she was kind enough not to break out in a loud laugh.

"You need to call a veterinarian's office for that. We are the Veterans Administration Office," she added. But she wouldn't tell me how the word was spelled. For that matter, she also didn't tell me what a Veterans Administration office was. I'd have to learn that the same way I learned everything else in this new language, the hard way.

That little episode reminds me of other struggles with language and culture that I have had to confront over the years. One such was the first time I went to a grocery store in the States. A lady asked me, "How are you today?" Having a bad headache that morning I replied, "I have such a headache, I could scream."

She gave me a bewildered look, as if to say, "That was more than what I wanted to hear."

I could tell that she was not really interested in how I was, and I didn't understand why she would ask such question if she didn't want the answer. If a German asks how you are, you tell the truth. That's probably why most Germans don't often ask a stranger that question. Instead, a German greeting is more like to be a "good morning" or "good day" which is what Americans often mean when they ask, "How are you." It's not actually a question. It's a greeting. I also quickly learned – and sometimes painfully -- that jokes, colloquialisms, sayings, and many forms of family or office shorthand were often not translatable.

Another of these incidents colors my memory of that first "cold shoulder" meeting with Wes' mother. On that first long drive across the United States we had, as noted earlier, stopped in Ohio to visit Wes' aunt. Hers was a warm welcome. But she had some unique quirks. One of these was her habit of giving everything in the house a name. A door might be "Mike." A carpet might be "Willy." Her list of such names was long, so it's no surprise that Wes didn't notice when one of these was about to cause me embarrassment later on our trip.

One evening, after a dinner at home with Aunt Dottie, I wanted to pitch in and help clean up. As we were in the kitchen, I asked, "What do you do with the scraps on the plates?"
"Oh, we give them to George," Aunt Dottie answered.

I look around to see where George was. Or who George was.

She saw me searching and pointed into the kitchen sink, "There's George," she said, "he takes care of the garbage."

Suddenly there was a gurgling, whirring sound. George was the garbage disposal. I had never seen a garbage disposal.

In fact, I didn't know such things existed. In my German villages of Kleinforst, Wohnroth, and Hirschfeld, if we had left over dinner scraps, we'd feed them the pig or to the chickens.

Wes had heard the exchange with his aunt, but it didn't occur to him then that Aunt Dottie had just planted the seed to a future embarrassing moment.

That moment occurred – you guessed it – after we reached California. At our first dinner with Wes' mother, I again wanted to be helpful. Off to the kitchen I went to help scrape plates and wash dishes. Looking into the sink, I said to Wes' mother, "Oh, so you've also got a 'George.'"

She had not the foggiest idea what I was talking about.

"A what?"

I began to suspect something was wrong.

"A George, for the garbage."

"You mean the garbage disposal? Why on earth would anyone be stupid enough to call it a George?"

So now you know. Learning a new language has its pitfalls.

After six months in Greenland, Wes came home on leave for Christmas. We had a wonderful time. The kids loved to have their Dad home again. The 30 days leave flew by like a hurricane. It seemed that he had been home only for a week instead of four. To leave again after the holidays was extremely hard for him and almost broke his heart. It was still 24-hour darkness in Greenland and there were extreme weather conditions. The adjustment for both of us was extremely difficult. I once again felt very much alone.

We decided I should become an American citizen while he was in Greenland since his next assignment was to be Berlin, Germany. The Cold War was at its height, and for us to travel from Berlin to West Germany to visit my parents and brothers would be a big hassle, and even dangerous since I originally came from East Germany. My German passport still showed Kleinforst as my place of birth. East German border guards would see one German – born in the East -- and three Americans in the car. That would have been cause for additional questioning and delays by the East German guards.

So I took an American history class, passed my test, and in Denver, Colorado, became an American citizen. I missed Wes so much the day of the naturalization. I wanted to share this special day with him while taking the oath before a judge.

It was not easy to give up my citizenship. I had mixed emotions. On the one hand I was excited to become an American. On the other I felt like I was a traitor to my country. Several immigrants who stood in front of the judge and who were called to step forward broke down at the last minute and couldn't do it. The scene almost took my breath away. I had to stay strong so I wouldn't do the same.

An American in Germany

In the summer of 1975 Wes returned from Greenland. We were a happy family again and packed our bags for the next Germany assignment. As it turned out, his posting to Berlin had been cancelled. Instead he was to report to Ramstein Air Base. It didn't matter to me as long as it was Germany. We would be going home. I could visit my family again. I had missed so much of their lives.

When we arrived at the Rhein Main airport I began to have mixed emotions. We had crossed the Atlantic Ocean again. This time we had headed toward Germany and home. Was I now an American after having lived nine years in the U.S., or was I still a German? How would I be accepted by the Germans? As a traitor who had given up her citizenship? In any case I was happy to be back in my homeland for a few years.

In the Ramstein area, less than an hour from that little village of Hirschfeld, we rented the third floor of a house owned by an elderly German couple. It was in a very small village called Schrollbach. Our apartment had three bedrooms and 22 windows which surrounded the entire third floor. The kids took the school bus daily into Ramstein, a distance of about 4 miles. Things were going great. Wes loved his job. He worked as a public affairs officer at HQ, United States Air Force in Europe.

The Cold War was still in full swing, and the importance of the troops in Germany was critical.

Once settled, I found I wasn't able to work as a beautician since I didn't have a German license. So I decided, since I now had American citizenship, to apply on the air base for a federal service clerical position. And thus began my career working for the American Federal Government.

I started as a clerk typist in the Standardization and Evaluation Directorate of Operations of the United States Air Forces in Europe. My office was in the headquarters building across the street from the Officers Club. My job was to type reports from instructor pilots who evaluated the fighter pilots.

It was strange. Wes was using my language for his Community Relations work in public affairs, and I was using his language to edit and correct work done by American college graduates. My dictionary was put to use on a daily basis. When I didn't know a word that I was typing, I would look it up to find out if the spelling was correct. At the same time I'd learn the meaning of the new word.

After a year I moved to a secretary position in the Command Post Directorate and often substituted for the secretaries in the Generals' offices upstairs. The generals liked my work and my work ethics. The tumbleweed was beginning to show signs of life.

When not working, we traveled throughout Europe, visited my parents and relatives and enjoyed our kids. When school was out, Iris and Eric got to do something they never could while in the States. They could go for summer visits to their German grandparents. Their U.S. grandparents, having rejected me, had never been a factor in their lives.

With both of us working, the Ramstein years were the first time in our lives that we didn't have to struggle financially as hard as we had in the past. Wes extended his assignment for a second three-year posting at Ramstein, for a total of six years.

Life was good until one day in December of 1979. One Saturday, I returned from a shopping trip to Kaiserslautern. Christmas was only weeks away, and we had plans to travel to northern Germany to spend the holidays with my family. But when I arrived home from my shopping, Wes was gone. The kids were crying that Daddy had to leave.

"Where did he go?" I asked.

"We don't know, he couldn't say. He just left," they cried.

It was about two weeks before Christmas. I was devastated. I called his office. The only thing they could tell me that he was on Temporary Duty to an undisclosed location. The Middle East at that time was a hot spot owing to the Iranian crisis, among other things. Perhaps he was there I thought.

I was working for the Command and Control Directorate having received a promotion. The Command Post was in our directorate, but even they were not able, or permitted, to tell me his whereabouts. It was Top Secret. They could only tell me that he was fine but that was all.

One day, I received a phone call from someone in the Command Post. I was told to buy some work uniforms for him and leave them in front of their door. They would assure he would get them. With the suitcase of uniforms I enclosed a picture of us. He had travelled many times on Air Force duty, but this was different. He and his "deployment bag" had vanished.

I found myself a German married to an American, living in Germany, working on an American base for the U.S. government, mother of two American children attending American school, and suddenly awful lonely. I added up all the time that I had been alone during his AF career up to then. It came to four years: One year here, three months there, and so on.

The kids and I spent that 1979 Christmas with my parents, not knowing where Wes was. Three months had passed when I received a phone call saying I could pick him up at the flight line. He had finally returned. He still couldn't tell me where he had been until many years later when it became unclassified.

It turned out his temporary duty was somewhere in Egypt where the Air Force had set up a temporary base. He was among the group who made the preparations for a rescue operation, Operation Eagle Claw, which took place on April 24, 1980. The operation itself was many weeks after Wes returned to Ramstein. Unfortunately, it resulted in a failed mission, the destruction of two aircraft and the death of eight American servicemen and one Iranian civilian. It was an embarrassment for the U.S. and for President Jimmy Carter.

After the event, the morale of the airmen was at its lowest. Wes, walking the streets of Ramstein Air Base, was embarrassed to look into the eyes of other NATO officers he encountered. It was a hard time for him.

Just months following that operation, the U.S. had a new President, the hostages in Iran had been released, and we had orders to depart Ramstein. Our six-year posting to Germany had come to an end. The tumbleweed would once again hop the Atlantic. My homeland, my family, my employment – all once again relegated to the pages of a scrapbook. The next barbed-wire fence to snag this tumbleweed would be in the state of Indiana.

A Tumbleweed Takes Root

Wes was assigned to Fort Harrison in Indianapolis as a Public Affairs Instructor at the Defense Information School. At first I was not crazy about moving to Indianapolis. We had lived in the city for three months in 1970 when Wes attended the same school just after his commission to lieutenant.

Indianapolis had seemed a small "cow town," just the kind of place tumbleweeds might truly call home. Years later I learned to love the city. Downtown was revitalized. Basketball was "hot," new stadiums were built for NFL, basketball and baseball teams, and of course the Indy 500 was growing having added two additional races. New hotels and shopping malls opened up, and the arts were expanded. Indianapolis had become metropolitan.

But as we had departed the city after our first brief stay in Indianapolis, we left with a sour taste in our mouths. We were faced with driving to Montana after Wes completed his course, and we desperately needed new tires on our car. We didn't have a credit card we could use for the tires. We had always depended on Sears or Household Finance for credit. So in a crunch we applied at a local Indianapolis bank.

The bank denied us the credit because Indiana wasn't our home state, and we were in transit. Our credit worthiness was not an issue. Again, as often happens to military members, we felt isolated. So in 1981, as we were establishing our new Indianapolis household just blocks from that very bank, we did not open an account there. Nor did we seek a mortgage there for the new home we bought in Indianapolis.

I did not know it as we settled into Indianapolis, but here the tumbleweed would take root. It would stay put nearly three decades and thrive even without the support of a rusty fence. But it would also weather its most ferocious storms, and that's not a reference to Indiana's well-known tornados.

All of the post-war hardships, the fears of Russian soldiers and communist neighbors, the risks of escape, the privations of refugee camps, the struggles for acceptance in new surroundings, the learning of a new language and a new culture, a hot bullet in Ohio, and a cold shoulder in California – all of this had been preparation for the battles I would have to fight in Indianapolis.

What I "brought to the table" as I began life in Indiana was a well-honed approach to facing adversity. I would face hurdles, obstacles, challenges, resistance, and bureaucratic barriers. In fact, these would be the norm, not the exception.

But for me, to be denied an opportunity is not a time to stomp on the brakes! Just the opposite. I go for the accelerator. Where others see the red flag of denial, I see the green flag of the Indianapolis 500. Engines roar, earth trembles, birds fly off in terror, and I'm off on a race to the checkered flag!

I turned the first "red flag" green when I applied for my first job in Indiana. I arrived with a large manila envelope stuffed with evidence of my experience. At Ramstein I had started as a clerk and quickly advanced to highly-trusted secretarial work at the top level of Air Force command in Europe. There I was often called upon to work for the Generals when their own secretaries were on vacation. The Generals liked the trip books I prepared for them and the correspondence I typed for their signatures.

Since we didn't have computers yet at that time, accuracy was of utmost importance. Yet despite that experience, when I sought employment in Indianapolis the first hurdle was the Federal Civil Service office itself.

"You have just three months," I was informed, "and if you have not secured a Federal position by then, we'll have to revert you to 'new applicant' status."

And, not surprisingly, that was followed with, "We have no openings for you here in Indianapolis."

Was that one "red flag" or two? It must have been two, because within one month, I found an opening in Greenwood, Indiana, an hour's drive to the south. I applied, went to an interview, and accepted a position with the Army Corps of Engineers – a Federal civil service job.

It was a notch or two below what I had been doing for the Air Force in Germany, and it was a lengthy commute, so I kept that "bird in the hand" for a year while still searching for a more suitable position closer to home.

I submitted applications at Fort Harrison, which was the Indianapolis base where Wes worked. Time and again, I got the response, "You are 'outside the system' which meant nothing more than 'we hire only insiders'."

Finally after several rejections, Wes – in his Air Force uniform – physically took my application, sat calmly but sternly looking into the eyes of a clerk in civilian personnel, and handed her my application.

"Yes, Major," the clerk said. "I'll see to it."

Shortly thereafter, I was placed on the "interview list" and soon found myself working on Fort Harrison in the military hospital.

Two years later I was ready for something more challenging, and Wes was approaching retirement. He had enjoyed his job as an instructor teaching about Western Europe and the Soviet Union, and we felt quite at home in Indiana. So we decided to stay in Indianapolis.

Wes had just about completed his master's degree at Butler University, and he was hoping to find a local civilian teaching position. Of interest to me, there was an opening on Fort Harrison for a civilian "training technician." The job was within the Defense Information School, and my administrative experience was a good match for the requisite skills of that job. I applied.

"Sorry," came the response. "Can't hire you. Nepotism laws won't permit you to apply."

Two hurdles in one sentence. Nepotism was a vocabulary challenge. An English word this tumbleweed had not yet encountered. It sounded like some sort of disease. Next, there was the word "law" about nepotism. Looked like another "green flag" to me. Off to the races!

Once I learned that nepotism was a policy prohibiting the hiring of family members into the same organization, I set out to navigate past that roadblock. I knew what the Defense Information School didn't know. Wes would soon be retiring. He had already begun to make plans for a new career in civilian life. For 21 of his nearly 24 years in the Air Force, he had attended night schools and had completed three degrees: one in English, another in German, and a Masters in Radio and TV. His goal was to become a school teacher after his Air Force retirement, a dream he had had since I met him.

So with Wes retiring, and nepotism no longer an issue, I found myself employed in the same school and the same directorate as he had been. I became a training technician, similar in some respects to secretarial work, but with greater focus on training programs and educational events.

My federal employment seemed secure. Wes was hired locally as a middle school teacher, teaching English and German, so our stay in Indianapolis looked more permanent. It was, in fact, more permanent. But the tumbleweed's challenges and hurdles were far from over.

After advancing well as a training technician, I began to notice that there were higher paying positions for which I was clearly qualified. Not only that, but I was already performing most of the very tasks that went with those positions. So I applied for promotion.

On cue, up came the roadblocks. I was asked to write a series of documents called KSA's – Knowledge, Skills, Abilities. This seemed fair enough until I found that others applying for similar positions were not asked to do so. Then I was asked to re-classify the positions and write detailed job descriptions. Another task not required of other applicants for similar jobs. Finally, I was asked to produce documentation to validate and justify savings to the organization's budget to be realized by my advancement. I became incensed when it became clear that advancement policies were inconsistently applied among applicants for various positions.

At about the same time, I learned that the organization itself – Defense Information School – was soon to be closed locally and only a relative few of the civilians would be transferred to a new location in another state.

It was time for the tumbleweed to seek another barbed-wire fence. I applied for, interviewed, and was accepted for an administrative position in another organization on Fort Harrison. The Army Finance Center was not slated to close or move. So, my career – like the rest of my life to date – had only one constant, and that was change.

Once at work in my new office, I soon found two new obstacles to "success in the American workplace." One, as I had learned waitressing in Montana, is that all too often co-workers resent those who go beyond "the requirements." Another is that envious "colleagues" are likely to spend more time "back-stabbing" the competition than they devote to doing their own jobs.

In my new job at the U.S. Army Information Systems Command, I adhered to my habit of always finding something useful to do during "slow times" between major projects. I'd replenish supplies, arrange and label files, update contact lists, or organize published directives.

I would do these things simply because they needed done. My co-workers, however, seemed to think my goal was to make them look lazy or inefficient. The fact that most of them took regular "smoke breaks" outside the office while I did not, added to their resentment. It was like union workers bristling in anger at those who exceed the hourly quota.

When I started my job in that office I was given the task to coordinate our Information Systems Command's Closing Ceremony, a task normally given to military members and Protocol personnel. It involved requesting award citations from various division supervisors for military and civilian personnel, developing the invitational flyer and sending it out to guests, developing the program, coordinating with the Officer's Club for the reception and the placing of flags, locating an emcee. Military award citations had to be forwarded to HQ. In other words I planned and coordinated the entire ceremony.

Once the Base Commander, one-star general, found out that a secretary was performing this task, he immediately ordered through his Chief of Staff a dry-run of the program. During the ceremony, the Chief of Staff sat four rows in front of me. He turned his head and gave me thumbs up. He was happy that everything went that well. My supervisor on the other hand never thanked me for a job well done.

Outright envy also played a role in souring the work climate after I started my new job. Unknown to me, another office member had applied for the job for which I was hired. In her eyes, I was the "outsider" who took a job she felt was hers to have. Once, several months after I started, I put together a detailed and complex travel itinerary for my boss. There were airplane tickets, taxis, rental cars, hotels, and various meetings involved. This sort of planning was routine for me because I had done far more complex arrangements for special events in my previous jobs. All of the details for my boss' trip were ready and completely annotated in a special travel folder I had prepared for her. It happened that I would be out on vacation myself during the boss' travel, so I had double-checked every detail.

In my absence the envious co-worker – we'll call her "Brandy" – added her own special touch to the boss' itinerary. Brandy cancelled a key airport shuttle reservation (I was later able to verify this). And somehow the entire folder, with all of its carefully annotated contact information on the inside cover, mysteriously disappeared. As a result, the boss was late to an important meeting, and I received a harsh lambasting.

Ultimately, my boss so severely and so publicly maltreated me that I had no choice but to officially initiate harassment proceedings. I won the case. In compensation, the commission required my boss herself to find a new position for me. She did, and the tumbleweed next snagged a fence, still at Fort Harrison, at the Army Finance School.

More lessons on "success in the American workplace" awaited me at my new job. My new supervisor, an Army Executive Officer to the Finance School Commander, I learned some weeks later, had received advance warning that I was a "trouble-maker." Once I had settled into my new office, I learned that there was no specific job description for the position, and the workload was next to non-existent. I saw this as an opportunity to complete a course I had been selected for some time earlier. I had been taking daily one-hour classes to professionalize my secretarial skills. Once completed the course would lead to "certified secretary" credentials. There had been little if any negative impact on my office since the courses amounted to using an "extended lunch period" in a classroom environment.

My new supervisor's response? "Denied." He told me I could not continue the course owing to my current workload. No sooner had he denied my application for that training than yet another lesson on "success in the American workplace" came my way.

Some supervisors who wish to rid themselves of "troublesome" employees will resort to tasking the employee with an unattainable project and then documenting the employee's failure to complete assigned work.

I could not prove such intent in a legal hearing, but consider this. I was a trained administrative assistant. In short, a clerical secretary. My new supervisor, the Commander's Executive Officer, came to me one Friday with these instructions, "The Commander needs to make a speech on the topic of 'change' and he needs to present the speech Wednesday. He'll need the completed speech on his desk

Monday. I'm assigning you the task since your work load is light at this time."

I gave some sort of non-committal response, and he left. I had just been given a recipe for failure. I was so new, I had no idea who the "Commander" was, much less what he would want to say about "change." More to the point, I was not a trained speech writer. My supervisor was the Commander's Executive Officer and qualified for such a task, not me. But, I am nothing if not resourceful.

What my supervisor did not know was that among the "cards in my hand" was an ace he was not aware of. Nor did he know that he had just dealt me two additional aces. The first ace was – you guessed it – my husband, Wes. While the tumbleweed had zero experience writing speeches, Wes was an accomplished writer. He had written for newspapers, magazines, Air Force history books, and, yes, even speeches for Air Force commanders. He also understood why my supervisor had given me the task.

The other two aces? Well, my supervisor had just given me a tip. He had confirmed a rumor that had been circulating around the base. The "change" the commander was to speak about was the forthcoming relocation of all of the training units on Fort Harrison leaving only the Finance Center on the post.

The second ace? I knew it was time for this tumbleweed to seek Federal employment outside the base.

To say that my supervisor was surprised to find the speech on his desk that Monday morning would be something of an understatement. And it was a good speech! Wes had made a few "contacts" and had correctly identified both the audience and the purpose of the speech. And I had just converted another "red" flag into a "green" flag.

The Commander called me in his office. He wanted to see for himself who this secretary was who wrote his speech, and who supposedly was such a trouble maker. He smiled when he greeted me and thanked me for the speech. I explained to him that I was not qualified for such a task but I knew how to find the right resources. He seemed very impressed with my resourcefulness and determination. I never heard his speech delivered, and to this day I don't know if he used it. My task was done. I couldn't be defeated.

Career Change

Fort Harrison was indeed about to close. The Department of Defense moved the schools and units to various other locations. In order for me to continue in the federal service, I had to find another job and do it before the avalanche of applications would burst forth. I was fortunate. My application reached the desk of the Indiana office of the U.S. Department of Commerce in April of 1993. I was hired as a secretary. The tumbleweed snagged what would be the final location in my quest for employment. The Director liked me immediately. He liked my motivation, and my history of outstanding performances. He turned out to be a great boss who understood my potential and provided opportunities for advancement. I was 48 years old and my professional-level career was just about to begin.

I moved from a secretary's position to a Trade Reference Assistant and from that to an International Trade Specialist within three years. The work was new, exciting and challenging. Because I knew I lacked the standard credentials required for the position (Undergraduate/Master's Degree), I worked at 200% tempo and climbed the ladder the hard way eventually reaching a GS-13.

That diminutive German girl who once sat on a bench and dreamed about where that highway just outside the village of Hirschfeld might lead was now offering "value added export counseling" to the CEO's of Indiana manufacturing and export-ready companies.

I had to know product applications and end-users of products ranging from pancake mix, to high tech machines to nuclear waste management. I worked on a daily basis with my colleagues located overseas in U.S. embassies. Together we would seek foreign markets and business partners for my Indiana clients.

I participated in overseas trade missions. I planned and coordinated and even made oral presentations to international trade seminars and conferences. I traveled to places like Mexico and Italy, and found myself working in cities like Chicago, Dallas, and Washington, D.C.

Climbing this ladder to an International Trade Specialist was not an easy task. Yes, my first supervisor saw my potential, but some of the higher ups were not supportive of my advancement. Neither was my second supervisor.

The question of my credentials came into play every time I competed for a promotion based on my work performance. I exceeded goals that even existing trade specialists with university degrees could not or did not meet. Other trade specialists saw me as a threat to their positions. More than once my efforts were sabotaged, such as when co-workers deleted my client data base.

Half of my data base "disappeared" from the server, and since I did not have access to the server, I could not have erroneously erased my own client list. Interestingly enough, only my client files disappeared, not those of other trade specialists.

Another method of sabotaging my efforts became apparent when a supervisor assigned my "industry sector" to another trade specialist and gave me a less lucrative list. On the surface this might have looked like a simple internal reorganization of responsibilities. But, in reality, what it meant was that I had painstakingly developed a solid base of productive exporting clients. This was taken from me and handed intact to someone else, while I received a new industry sector with an undeveloped client list.

Yes, I was angry and offended. But it was just another red flag which I turned to a green flag.

Bullying was also common during that time. We now had access to the Internet, and one of my colleagues was tasked to create a website for our office. Since I declined to have my picture on the official site, which was optional, this individual posted a drawing of a witch riding a broom. After I threatened him with a defamation of character suit, he removed the witch picture from the site. Eventually the individual was fired. For what reasons, I don't know.

"You are setting the standards too high for us," I was told by my colleagues.

"Keep focused only on your clients," Wes would tell me over and over again. "They are the ones that count."

Occasionally my clients would ask me during my office visits or when I was making presentations, "What keeps you so motivated as a government employee?   Wouldn't you rather come and work for us in the private sector?"

It was a compliment to me, but in the "ears" of my fellow trade specialists, such comments fomented envy.

I stayed focused on my clients. I worked hard for them and celebrated with them every time they entered a new overseas market. We were given performance quotas. These I exceeded every year.

"I was called the Unsung Hero" by our Headquarters in Washington, was named Trade Specialist of the Region, received accolades from Commercial Officers overseas and CEOs and company presidents in my client territory.   Every such success was hard fought and always included overcoming barriers of language, education, and culture. At every turn, I faced adversity that often seemed overwhelming and insurmountable.

A lady came from Washington DC arrived in our office to get a statement from me in reference to a discrimination suit.

A colleague who had been passed over for promotion filed a complaint against me. She was envy that I had been promoted but she hadn't. She says I was evil and discriminated against her because she was black. She hoped I would get fired. This colleague hadn't come to work for about a year on a regular basis. The boss couldn't do anything about this. He had to document the situation before taken action. She had been influenced by three other coworkers who also wanted me to be out of the office. Those individuals eventually were either fired or left on their own. I was shocked when I heard of these accusations. She forgot however, that she wrote me a beautiful letter some time back after I helped her to enter the professional career path, as well as provided her with household items. She was a single mother and needed help.

She wrote: *"Josie, We've come a long way with this relationship of ours: Many have touched the edges of my life...coming and going, scarcely leaving a positive impression at times. But you are an uncommon person, someone who has made a difference in my life. Although forced to grow up sooner than most, I've realized I still have yet to experience life for what it really is. You've helped me find ways to work through some problems that otherwise might have made me give up or go in a different direction than what's best for me. I admire you in ways words can't express. You are a role model as a parent, as a wife, as a colleague, as a "survivor" and a genuine friend. It's people like you who make the difference in this "crazy" world though you may not hear it often, you are very much appreciated and will never be forgotten. I only hope that I can be as impressionable to you as you've been to me. With deepest love and appreciation."*

As it turned out this colleague left the service and received a retirement. She had no case.

I survived another bullying.

But just as I was launching this new Commerce Department career, I had found myself facing yet another challenge. I was in this new job for only two months, when my life-or-death struggle began. It began right where this book began, with that phone call, the broken chair, and Wes' solo trip to do what he could to help Mutti and Vati.

Conquering Cancer

Wes returned home and was anxious to see what the problem was with me. I had made my doctor's appointment while he was gone to speed things up. The doctor examined me and sent me immediately to the Breast Diagnostic Center for a mammogram. He didn't say much but was concerned enough to have me immediately further tested without scheduling another appointment. During the mammogram I felt a slight tingling in my left breast. Being technically challenged, I thought that it might be too much radiation penetrating through my breast. My breast was compressed on the cold plate of the unit until it looked like a pancake. The pain was almost unbearable. This procedure had to be done that way to increase image quality by reducing the thickness of breast tissue that x-rays must penetrate. It was repeated from various angles producing about six images for each breast.

"We'll need to do an ultrasound," the nurse said. "Let's go to another room. The physician will do that," she continued but didn't say anything else.

I lay on the table and started to shiver. It wasn't the air conditioning causing this. It was my nerves playing tricks on me. My imagination went on overdrive. I saw myself dying right here on the table. The doctor performing the ultrasound was quiet but looking at the monitor very intensely. She turned the monitor so I could see it from the bed and showed me a large white spot.

"I'll be sending you back to your doctor's office," she said without any attempt at diagnosing the problem. "You may need additional referrals."

I wasn't able to see my physician right away, but the nurse told me that she would schedule an appointment with my surgeon who had removed my gallbladder just three months prior. She said she'd let me know of the time of the appointment. I didn't know why I had to see my surgeon since no one had yet given me a diagnosis.

The appointment with the surgeon was scheduled for two days later, on a Friday. He looked at the mammogram x-rays and said, "This doesn't look good. I don't like the calcification concentrated in one area. The ultrasound shows a large mass." He was looking at a black and white image while he was talking to me.

"I recommend a lumpectomy and biopsy," the surgeon continued. "Let's schedule you for Monday morning for surgery. If I have to, I'll reschedule my other surgery for that morning. We need to get you in as early as possible. Is 6 a.m. too early for you?"

All I had heard was the word surgery and nothing else. I was in shock. The weekend was hell. I couldn't think, eat or sleep. Anxiety had taken control of every fiber of my being.

The surgery went well.   When I woke up, Wes stood next to my bed.   His eyes were filled with tears. I knew immediately what that meant.

"I have breast cancer.   That is why you are crying. Right?"

He nodded.

"I will fight this SOB. It will not get me," I cried, still affected by the anesthesia.

"Dr. B. has removed a large malignant tumor and surrounding tissue," Wes continued.

But I didn't hear much of what Wes said after that. I had gone numb. Cancer! The word in my native language is "*Krebs*." It sounds no better in German than in English. I had known people who had had Krebs. None of them were still living.

"He will meet with us once you have recuperated from this surgery. Once the biopsy results are in. Then we'll discuss further steps."

My daughter Iris and her husband Lew were still stationed in Germany as I came out of that surgery. She was six months pregnant. She had had two prior miscarriages. The last miscarriage was only eight months ago. They had been married for seven years and we, like they, were happy that this time she might be able to carry it through. We knew it would be a little boy.

Wes and I, however, were in agony over whether to tell Iris about my situation. We feared another miscarriage and were tormented. But we agreed it wouldn't be fair not to tell her. It was the right thing to do. Even though it meant she would almost certainly head straight for the airport. Which is exactly what she did. As did our son Eric in California.

At the time of our daughter's second miscarriage, one 9th grader in Wes' English class noticed that her teacher was not as chipper as usual and asked him if he felt okay. Surprised by the question, he shared the news with her. The next day the little girl comforted him with a card. Inside she wrote, "Mr. Tilton, when God has a purpose for your grandchild, he will allow you to have one." Wes was blown away with the wisdom of a 9th grader, not realizing at that moment that a purpose and a grandchild was just a few months away.

Iris and Lewis arrived within 48 hours from Germany on an emergency leave flight while Eric arrived the day after my lumpectomy from his home on the West Coast. We all gathered around a conference table in the surgeon's office a few days later. There we were given the details.

"I have good news and I have bad news," my surgeon said. "The bad news is that you have a very aggressive type of cancer."

At this point I went numb. My whole body felt like my cheek and gums at a dentist office – moments after the

Novocain. It was as if I was there but not there. Most of what I know of the rest of that conference table meeting came from Wes, Iris, and Eric. What a blessing all three were there.

"You have an infiltrating ductile carcinoma which is invasive," the surgeon had said. "The good news is that this type of very aggressive tumor tends to respond to treatment very well. I have sent samples of the lumpectomy tissue to a lab in San Diego for further diagnosis," he continued. "Once that's in, we can set you up with oncology."

"Oncology. Another new word. The struggle continues," I thought. In this case, had I heard it in German I'd have been no better off. Only those who had been diagnosed with *"Krebs"* would have encountered the German word, *"Onkologie."*

"You will require another surgery to remove your lymph nodes since they are enlarged."

More new vocabulary. Lymph nodes. Now I was beginning to feel like a high school freshman attending a college course. My mind was spinning.

But I must have had a moment of clarity at some point in that discussion, because I remember asking, "Did I get the breast cancer because I took Estrogen and Progesterone for four years?" Something I had read about those hormones had triggered my question. "I don't have breast cancer in the family."

"It isn't fully proven yet whether the drugs cause breast cancer," Dr. B said. "If you have a pre-disposition to have cancer, however, those drugs could increase the risk."

I sat at the table and cried. I could not comprehend that I had cancer. I remembered my grandmother who had had cancer. It was a death sentence in those days. Dr. B. cried with me. I had never seen a Dr. cry in front of his patients. This showed a sensitivity of his character that warmed me. All these years later I still admire him for that. Many months after this meeting, on a follow-up visit, I gave him one of my paintings. It was a watercolor I had done not knowing whether or not he would keep it. To my surprise I learned 17 years later, when Wes was in the hospital due to a complication from a procedure he had had, that Dr. B still had the painting. Dr. B had been called to consult on Wes' problem. That's when I met him again. He recognized me right away and was thrilled that I had survived my stage III cancer. He stepped away but said he would come right back. When he returned he had the painting in his hand.

"I have kept this painting in my office all these years," he said. "I tell my patients where it came from all the time, and now I can also let them I know that it came from a 17-year survivor. That'll give them hope."

A month after we left that initial conference table, my second surgery revealed that six of 13 lymph nodes were positive. Several tumors had already broken through the node capsules. The cancerous nodes alone were described as level II, and with the size of the tumor, my overall cancer was diagnosed as level III. The cancer was systemic. He ordered more tests, such as liver blood test, chest x-ray and bone scan to find out if the cancer had metastasized anywhere else.

Dr. B. left the decision up to me if I wanted to have a modified radical mastectomy, or if I wanted to pursue a course of chemotherapy and radiation. He emphasized that the cancer was already in the blood stream due to the size of the breast tumor – comparable to a small chicken-egg -- and the number of lymph nodes involved.

"I can't explain why some women opt for a radical mastectomy and others don't," he said.

At this second "conference table meeting," we as a family were better equipped to grapple with the information. Wes and Eric in particular had attacked books and articles like they were prepping for a master's thesis. Iris and I had had time to "process" and were of a more positive frame of mind. The numbness had faded. The "red flag" was about to be replaced with green. I was nearly ready for engines to roar, earth to tremble, birds to fly off in terror.... I was once again about to be off on a race to the checkered flag! But first, there was more to learn from my surgeon, and soon from – we had learned the new word – my oncologist.

"According to my statistics, the cancer could come back whether you have a breast or not," Dr. B continued. "I believe that some women choose the mastectomy thinking that with the breast gone, so is the risk of recurrence. But a risk of recurrence is still there," he continued.

Iris was still with us at home and together we awaited the results of the tests. My nerves were at the end. I couldn't sleep or eat as a result of the anticipation over the outcome of these tests. One afternoon Iris and I went to a local book store to find some books about chemotherapy. I asked her to skim through since I didn't have the courage. I really didn't want to know all the side effects and risks that could happen during the treatment. She read enough to ease her own mind and told me that everything would be OK. Wes and Eric had read similar books, but I could not get past the word "statistics." I didn't feel like a statistic, and I did not want to be a statistic.

When we arrived home, Wes stood at the kitchen door holding a champagne glass in his hand. I knew right away that the test results had come in.

"All tests were clean. Dr. B. just called to let us know."

I was relieved, but only partially. I had that "hungry but not hungry" feeling in my stomach I had had at the time of our escape. Mutti, Vati, the train platforms. The cold. The whispering. A gnawing fear. So many things I did not at the time understand.

"No evidence of metastases to liver, lung or bones," Wes seemed more confident than he had been for many days. "This calls for a celebration," he said.

I cried like a little baby. It was such a relief. Although I had a long road ahead of me, I knew I could do it. I knew it was the green flag or nothing! A few days later Iris and Lew flew back to Germany. Eric had already returned to California.

In late August, 1993, we consulted with my oncologist, Dr. G. He confirmed stage III cancer because of the large tumor in my left breast and the six positive nodes in my left armpit. A tumor in one of the nodes had broken through the node capsule and was 2.3 cm, about an inch.

"The good news with all that is that this type of cancer responds to treatment very well," Dr. G. explained. My surgeon had said much the same thing, but now we had biopsy results confirming his suspicions.

"The bad news is that it is so aggressive that without any treatment, the chances for your survival would be no greater than 5%," he continued.

He had actually said "five-year survival," but either way, I saw myself with one foot in the grave. I felt like a statistic, cold and with all the feeling of a Popsicle.

He then outlined several chemotherapy treatments on his wall-mounted white board in the examination room and explained survival statistics of these various treatments. He seemed very cold not showing any emotions, totally opposite from Dr. B. He wasn't cold, as I later learned, but was actually very caring.

"I do not want to hear the statistics," I said. "I want to fight it on my own terms."

"Isn't every human being different? Aren't the effects different? " I asked.

I was beginning to grasp what Wes and Eric had been telling me about cancer survival statistics. Some of the numbers pertain to the overall group of those who have cancer. Other reports compare patients who have accepted treatment with those who chose no treatment at all. Of course, the 5% survival rate would be an outcome for the "no treatment" group. I had already decided I wasn't going to be in that group.

"That's fine with me," he said. "I won't go into detail on the stats."

I was beginning to feel like a person again.

"However, I would like to mention a clinical trial we have ongoing."

Another vocabulary hurdle, I thought.

"This is a program which includes four sessions of treatment with 21 to 28 day intervals. We'd be using an ultra-high dose of chemotherapy followed by – and this is the "why" of the clinical trial – a new drug to rapidly restore your white blood cells."

At this point, the tumbleweed had no idea why the white blood cells would need "restored." But what I had just heard had already convinced me. This clinical trial would be my best chance to avoid becoming one of those 95% do-nothing, non-survivors.

"The drugs are commonly used breast cancer drugs such as Adriamycin and Cytoxan" Dr. G went on. "We'll be using a much higher dose therapy than the standard dose."

I was beginning to see myself as a survivor.

"The study is designed to test whether higher than standard doses of chemotherapy, together with this new drug, are more effective than standard doses for curing and preventing breast cancer from coming back."

But then he hit me with another statistic.

"There is, however, a slight risk of developing leukemia, about 1%."

I let that one go. Wes and Eric had had some impact on my thinking with those numbers. Focus on the reverse. In this case, the 99% who would not develop leukemia.

"The goal of having four doses of this particular chemotherapy is this. We'll kill 90% of your cancer cells with the first dose. Then, in the next session, we kill 90% of the residual cancerous cells. We'll repeat this over the four sessions until the last cancer cell is destroyed."

That sounded good to me. I had just heard a goal, and it sounded achievable.

The new drug, later to be called Neupogen, had a name filled with vocabulary stumbling blocks. My oncologist called it, "granulocyte colony stimulating factor." His nurse called it "g-c-s-f." Either way, it was a mystery to me. Still, it seemed to offer hope. But my hope would soon be dashed. Or at least clobbered by a big rock, another stumbling block.

"We administer the 'granulocyte colony stimulating factor' for 10 days following each chemotherapy session," he continued. "It's a shot to bring back the white blood cell count," he concluded.

I agreed to go ahead with the trial. What was there to lose? I had a very aggressive cancer which needed to be dealt with right away. At least with the trial I had a chance for survival. I didn't want to be included in the statistics of women who did nothing. I was still young and had a life in front of me. My husband and kids needed me. Also God had a purpose. We had been reminded of that by one of Wes' students. He was giving us a grandson.

I wanted to see our grandson grow up. It was totally in God's hands, and I needed to trust him. I didn't know that soon God would reveal himself to me in a special way. At a time when I most needed him. Scripture tells us to "be still, and know that I am God." We also can read the story of Elijah when he found that God was not in the wind, or the earthquake, or even the fire. He is in "the still small voice of our hearts." He is speaking to us in ways we may not imagine, but he is speaking. Be still – it's a noisy world and he whispers.

Things for me were beginning to connect. I was born to a German Lutheran family, was baptized and confirmed but had not been practicing my religion for many years. I had been longing for a closer relationship to God for some time and had wanted to become a Catholic ever since I visited masses with my grandmother. Mama was Catholic. Wes, a Catholic in his childhood, had turned his back to the Catholic Church for various reasons, and so we stayed away from any religious institutions. That, too, was soon to change.

But my hope that this clinical trial would offer me life, including life to spend with grandchildren, began to fade with Dr. G's next comments.

"Because this is a clinical trial," he began to caution me, "I cannot guarantee you'll have the treatment. There is a random selection process."

I felt myself sinking.

"Then, if you are selected," he added, "you'll have to pass stringent tests, especially for your heart, to be sure you are physically capable of withstanding the stress."

The tumbleweed felt suddenly disoriented. It was as if the wind was blowing me over snowfields. Miles and miles of treeless snowfields. There was nothing to snag onto.

The Treatment

I was accepted for the clinical trial and soon thereafter underwent several other tests to see whether my body and my heart were strong enough to withstand the double-dose chemotherapy. My oncologist wrote the order calling for the four treatments. They'd be three weeks apart, a total of 12 weeks. Looking back, now, 12 weeks doesn't sound like much. Looking forward, then, those 12 weeks seemed an eternity.

The date for my first of four chemotherapy treatments was set for August 30, 1993. The afternoon before, on the 29th, Wes and I visited a local university park where we often walked. We sat on a small hill in front of a pond from which a large fountain shot its water into the air. We cuddled on the grass on this warm sunny day and silently observed the surrounding nature. I prayed that God would be with us on this journey. It was very peaceful.

The peaceful day turned painful very quickly. On our way home we stopped at a hairdresser shop to purchase a wig. I was about to become as bald as a grapefruit. The numbness of the whole ordeal returned with the force of a tsunami. Wes' eyes were tear-filled. The shop was a neighborhood beauty shop with little old ladies having their hair done. The owner of the shop knew right away why I wanted a wig and was very gracious and polite and didn't ask any questions. She directed us to a corner where several wigs filled a basket. All had been picked over by previous patients. I tried several of them on for fit when Wes lost it and walked out. It was too much for him to observe while I was trying on wigs. I found one and we drove away. This was the darkest day of my life.

We decided to have dinner at our local Chinese restaurant, about a ½ mile away from our house. It was a family style restaurant. The owners knew us, and I felt very comfortable there. When the fortune cookies arrived after dinner, I let Wes pick his and then I picked mine. No, I don't "believe in" fortune cookies, but it is always fun to read them. I opened up my cookie and couldn't believe what it said.

"It is always darkest just before the dawn." I agreed with it. "Wasn't this the darkest day of my life?"

Wes' cookie said something totally unrelated to our situation. I took my slip of paper home and glued it in a card I had received from Wes' colleague that said:

JESUS –
The Great Physician
He is watching over you,
Seeing to every detail.
He loves you,
In tenderness...

Compassion...

Gentleness.

He will do

His healing work.

How good it is to know

That you are under His special care.

The next day, August 30th, Wes took me to the first treatment at the Cancer Center. We briefly met with Dr. G. who went over the treatment plan again and explained what to expect. He wished me well.

The cocktail of my treatment was 102 mg of Adriamycin and 2050 mg of Cytoxin. The IV infusion lasted four hours while I was lying on a lounge chair, listening to soothing music that I downloaded onto my tape player. We didn't have iPods yet in those days. Wes read a book. But that didn't last long. His training was about to begin. My nurse approached him.

"Remember that 'g-c-s-f' the doctor told you about?"

"Sure," Wes answered. "Sounds like that is pretty much the key to this whole procedure. Dr. G said 'we administer that for 10 days after each session.' "

"That's right Kemo Sabe," she smiled tauntingly at Wes. Now, Wes is usually alert and quick on-the-draw with puns. But this one flew right past him, not to mention past me. But for me it was a cultural thing. Happens all the time. I had never heard of the Lone Ranger or his Indian sidekick, Tonto. But Wes' mind was saddled with thoughts of 'chemo' and life-and-death issues. Our nurse knew that. That's probably why she repeated it.

"You, Kemo Sabe, are the hand that turns the key to this whole procedure."

Wes seemed to see where this was going. At least his sense of humor began to resurface.

"Okay, Tonto," he said. "What is it you're trying to tell me?"

Wes caught-on and told the nurse he would always spell it "chemo sabe" from this point forward. Of course, at that point the tumbleweed had not the slightest clue what they were talking about. But something good had just happened. There were smiles and laughter. Things were looking up.

"You, Lone Ranger, are the 'we' who gives those shots of "g-c-s-f," our nurse told Wes.

I suddenly realized maybe I had the easy part. Wes' eyes were wide open at this point.

So, while I was connected to the four-hour IV flow of highly toxic chemotherapy drugs, Wes, himself a teacher, became a most attentive student. Our nurse began to train him how to give a shot. My Neupogen shots were to begin the next day and would continue for ten days to bring back the white blood cells. Wes was assigned to administer them.

"You'll be giving me a shot as your final test today," the nurse said to Wes.

"Me? I don't know if I can do that." Wes turned pale.

He didn't like to get shots himself and now he should give one to the nurse?

"Oh my," he said.

Laughingly she came with an orange in one hand and a syringe in the other.

"You can practice on the orange for a while before you give it to me," she said smiling. She demonstrated each step. Wes watched attentively.

Then she carefully watched as Wes gave the orange a shot in the flesh. He passed the test. She had him repeat the procedure. He punctured that orange three more times. His challenge then was to give the nurse a shot in her arm.

"It's just saline solution," she said. "Don't worry. It won't do me any harm."

A qualified shot giver was born. He didn't pass out.

The nurses in the facility were cheerful and happy, loved their jobs and made their patients as comfortable as possible. Our nurse, the one whose arm Wes punctured, was nothing shy of an angel. Make that A-n-g-e-l with a capital "A."

On the way out I noticed pictures of survivors. There was a collage hanging on a wall. Smiling faces seemed to reassure me that this can be beaten. This gave me a big sense of hope.

"You did well," the nurse said."

"We'll see you on your next treatment."

"This isn't so bad," I thought when we arrived at home.

I drank lots of water as directed and had a small meal. I practiced my positive thinking. I visualized that the drugs were attacking my cancer cells like Packmen that were gobbling up other little Packmen--one by one. I especially thought of my grandson who was to be born in December. I had to make it for him. God was sending him for a purpose just like the 9th grader had told Wes in school. His first purpose, still in the womb, was to give me the strength to make it through.

Now the long period of waiting began. Wes had returned to teaching. My parents and three brothers were living in Germany. Wes' family was scattered here and there. While Wes was teaching at the school, I sat alone at home, reading, watching TV or pursuing my art, at least after the first treatment. My appetite was not great, but I seemed to get some food down. After ten days, my hair was starting to fall out by the hand full. Instead of waiting for it to fall out completely, Wes decided to shave my head since what was happening was both fully predictable and unavoidable. We both stood in the bathroom and cried.

One of my neighbors came over several times. She had gone through cancer herself. Rose was 83. She offered to take me to the weekly blood tests at the Cancer Center which was only about three miles away. Rose and I became friends. Aside from Rose, I had only one close friend in Indianapolis, and she was still working. We had other friends, but they were scattered around the world as a result of our being in the Air Force. We hadn't had the chance to turn acquaintances into friendships in the time we had lived in Indianapolis. Besides, we both worked and didn't have much time for making friends or going to Church.

September 20th arrived and my second chemo treatment was about to begin. Up to that point my blood readings had been good, a sign of a healing body. This time I started without the inflammation around the breast and armpit surgery sites.

The day after that second chemo session Wes had to take me back to the Cancer Center. I had been vomiting a lot and was extremely dehydrated. The nurses put me on an IV and gave me Compazine and Ativan drugs to stop the vomiting. At home, Wes' training was again put in place. He administered my Neupogen shots to bring the white blood cell level back up. It had dropped to below 300 and needed to be at least 400 in order to receive the next chemotherapy treatment. After each dose, it was left to the doctor's discretion whether or not I was healthy enough to continue treatments.

Within three days of beginning those shots, the Neupogen started to kick in. I started to have lower back and thigh pains. It was a sign that the body was working overdrive to grow white blood cells. During the next three weeks before the next treatment, I sat mostly in my chair staring listlessly at the walls or at the TV. I no longer could read and comprehend nor paint my pictures. The cells in my body were being killed--- the good and the bad. That's what Dr. G had told us from the outset.

"The two drugs are indiscriminate. They kill blood cells. Red, white, and cancer cells," he had said.

I tried to imagine what my blood must look like. I thought it must be filmy and colorless, like milky liquid soap. I couldn't concentrate on anything except that I had to make it for my grandson. I barely could get any food down. A liquid energy and vitamin drink was all I could take in. My whole mouth felt painfully inflamed and foamy, sort of gummy, from the drugs.

My neighbor, Rose, brought me a sponge tooth brush so I could clean my teeth. My strength diminished. I barely could walk to the door to meet Rose to take me to the weekly blood tests.

As we got closer to the next treatment date, I was able to eat, but only a little. I craved Chinese food and so we decided to go back to our favorite Chinese restaurant to have dinner. At the end, we did our fortune cookie ritual again. Wes took his, and I took mine. I couldn't believe my eyes.

"You won't believe what my fortune cookie says," I said to Wes.

He was still unwrapping his cookie.

"This is unbelievable," I said. "Listen to this," and I read it to Wes.

It says, "You are more likely to give than to give in."

"Wow! Someone in the cookie factory knows you! How appropriate!" was Wes' response.

"I definitely won't give in. No matter how sick I am. What does yours say?" I asked.

"Nothing in particular," he answered.

I took mine home and pasted it in my card.

My blood count was up enough to receive my third treatment on October 11th. We knew now what to expect. The routine at the Center was the same. Only this time, I couldn't keep from vomiting during the treatment. The Ativan and Compazine weren't doing the trick any longer. Dr. G. came by and gave me some encouragement. He seemed a little more sympathetic towards me than he was during the initial counseling. Perhaps he could see that I was a fighter.

As with all of the chemo sessions—except for the time he was training with "the needle" – Wes sat next to me holding my "free" hand.

By the time the treatment was finished my vomiting stopped and we were able to go home.

We had to keep daily charts showing all manner of detail as part of the clinical trial. This was for statistical purposes.

Wes continued researching in the Cancer Society Book to see if there was anything else mentioned that we needed to know. I didn't have the courage to look inside the book.

Actually I couldn't bear to hear anything negative about breast cancer. It put me into a panic. All I wanted to hear were success stories. I contacted a local chapter of a breast cancer support group but never received a call back. So I decided to fight it alone and my way.

My strength diminished greatly after the third treatment. I barely made it to the door to greet Rose to take me for lab work. I was so sick and had lost already close to 30 pounds. Emotionally I was a wreck, and I didn't want to go on for the fourth treatment. Wes brought home one cold after another from his school classroom. His resistance was down due to the stress. I guessed that was why he was not able to shake the virus. I was lucky. Somehow, even with dangerously low white blood cell counts, I managed not to catch his viruses.

Nor did I get an infection from the chemo. I believe God was watching over me once again. My prayers were being answered.

I was too weak to go to our favorite restaurant just before the fourth and final treatment, so Wes went and brought the dinner home. The Chinese family didn't charge us for the dinner and they wished me well. What a warm and loving gesture that was. At home, we did our ritual with the cookies, mixing them this way and that to assure a random pick. Wes took his and I took mine. When I opened it, the message said:

"Move slowly but surely to success."

"This is impossible," I shouted. "How can this be?"

Every fortune cookie I had opened said something that was relevant to my situation. When you look death into the eye you cling to every sign that comes into your life. Were these signs? I wondered. "Was this a sign from God?" I asked Wes.

"I'm not so sure God and fortune cookies belong in the same sentence," Wes replied, a little uncomfortable with my question. We left the question at the table.

The fourth treatment day arrived on November 1st. My blood count was high enough to continue, although my strength was very weak.

"I can't do it anymore," I cried in the parking lot. "I am so exhausted, I can't do it."

"Yes you can," Wes replied. "Have you ever quit in your life? You are a fighter."

I didn't feel much like a fighter. I was exhausted.

"Look what you have accomplished in your life so far," Wes was trying to encourage me. "You've tumbled from East Germany to West Germany to the U.S. and you've faced every challenge head-on. You've struggled. And you've always made it."

Then he said the magic word. "And you've got a grandson coming. He's going to be born in Germany, in Rheinland Pfalz. Right where Iris was born!"

I opened the car door, and Wes helped me into the clinic.

"You are so close. Let's go."

The treatment was horrible. I vomited the entire time. The anti vomiting drugs didn't help much anymore. The four hours seemed like four days. My inner voice kept telling me to hang in there. The nurses gave me encouragement, and Wes sat next to me holding my hand as he had done during the first three chemo sessions. Dr. G. walked by and gave me thumbs up. He knew I would make it and felt proud of me.

The following three weeks were the worst. At home, I barely could get up from the chair. Opening the door to let Rose in was a marathon. I was out of breath just making two steps.

My whole body let me know that it had been hit very hard and didn't want any more. I sat in my chair and dreamed of my new grandson. I thought about how much I wanted to see him grow up. I focused on an image that I saw in the pattern of my coffee table leg. It's a huge oak table with legs nearly the size of a tree. In the wood grain I saw an image of a face. It was a little boy. Being an artist, I occasionally see images at different times, such as in clouds or in tiles on the bathroom floor. But this was remarkably calming. The pattern of the wood grain was my grandson's face!

Knowing that this was the fourth and last treatment gave me a small spur towards recovery. I gained a little more strength every day. Wes was making easy-to-digest but high protein meals for me. When anything called for milk, he'd mix powdered milk with the regular milk to boost its nutritional value. I was drinking fortified vitamin supplements. My goal was to be ready to have a nice big meal at Thanksgiving.

Despite the joy of having finished the treatments I now began to wonder if the chemotherapy worked. I am "Miss Anxiety" to all who know me well. And this time I felt justified at being anxious.

"How can we tell that the chemotherapy worked?" I asked Wes.

"We know you had the toughest chemo," he said, "not once but four times. Surely your cancer cells are gone with those treatments."

"I hope so," I said. But secretly I kept on praying to God to give me another sign to let me know that I was okay.

Slowly I was able to eat regular food again. Little by little I gained strength. After three weeks Wes and I decided to go to our Chinese restaurant. The restaurant was pretty crowded that night. I wore my wig so no one could see that I had cancer. After dinner we did our fortune cookie ritual once more. Wes took his and I took mine. A loud scream came out of my mouth:

"O my God."

"What's the matter?"

"I can't believe what I am reading on my fortune cookie."

"What is it?" Wes asked.

"Listen to this."

"Good health will be yours for a long time."

Tears were running down my checks. People started to look. I believed that God had answered my prayers. He had been with me the entire time. He revealed himself to me in whatever ways he could reach me, even if it was by means of a Chinese fortune cookie! I needed him. He found me! I am sure to this day that the cookies were his way of reaching me and bringing me closer to him.

I took my slip of paper home and pasted it into my card, still mesmerized by the four fortune cookies. "How could they have been so relevant to my four treatments?"

Wes' cookie, as had been the case each time, didn't say anything in particular. And that has also been the case with me from that point on. Whether we ate in that restaurant, or any other, my fortune cookies have never again been so strongly relevant to me. Think about it. Four cookies. Four chemotherapy treatments. And those cookies came in this succession:

"It is always darkest just before the dawn."

"You are more likely to give than to give in."

"Move slowly but surely to success."

"Good health will be yours for a long time."

Now, the last thing I want to do is start some new religious heresy. Wes and I talked about it, and we agreed: there is no magic in fortune cookies. But we also agreed that given our absence from any church activities, if God had wanted to reach me to give me hope and comfort, his chances of communicating with me were better via fortune cookies than with sermons.

Thanksgiving came. With Iris in Germany and Eric in California we knew not to expect family for the holidays. Wes took me out to eat that day. The food started to taste pretty good again. I was relieved to have made it through my four treatments.

But the challenges and hurdles were anything but over. Now was the time to get my strength back, but victory? Not yet! I next had to go through 28 rounds of radiation treatment. This was to start in January.

Still, things were looking up. Sunshine was beginning cast its rays back into my life. Our grandson, Lance, was born on December 15th. He was no longer an image on my wooden table, or a dream, or a hope. He was here! Iris and baby were fine, but they were also thousands of miles away. Lance had been born only a few miles from Hirschfeld, the very village where I lived those years after my family's escape from behind the Iron Curtain. What a miracle!!!! God was good to us once again.

God and Career

I went back to work at the beginning of December, to a job in the Commerce Department that I had scarcely had time to get familiar with. Now I could focus on a life beyond surgery, chemotherapy, doctors, nurses, and needles. Still, my radiation was scheduled for early January. The order called for 28 treatments not including weekends. It worked out that I could drive to the Cancer Center and receive the 5-minute treatment during my lunch hour. During the treatments while I was lying on the table, I focused on Iris' house in Germany. She had sent photos. I imagined walking through every room and visualized Lance, my beautiful grandson. This helped me to ignore the sound of the machine and kept me relaxed.

My boss at the Commerce Department was absolutely the best. He was the most considerate boss I had had in my entire federal career. He knew how anxious I still was – anxiety has always been my constant enemy -- so he decided to assign a big project to help me get my mind off the worries. The project was to coordinate a North America Free Trade Agreement (NAFTA) seminar. NAFTA had recently been adopted and details needed to be conveyed to the Indiana exporters. In March over three hundred people attended the event I had prepared. I was back in full swing with my work. My boss was very happy about the success and was reassured that he had made the right decision to move me from a Secretary to a Trade Reference Assistant earlier in April, one month after I had started at the office.

I had worked only for two months before my cancer diagnosis, and I was out of the office from August until December. I should mention two people, here, before moving on with the tumbleweed's story. One of them is Wes' brother in Green Bay, Wisconsin, and the other is an anonymous woman somewhere in Washington, D.C. Both of these dear people – in a sort of "Pay it Forward" mode – donated their own days of sick leave when I had exhausted my reserve.

I saw great opportunities for me in the Commerce Department office, and I was determined to reach the goal that I had envisioned, to become an International Trade Specialist despite my lack of "credentials."

My hard work paid off. I was promoted to an International Trade Specialist. A dream came true. I took Indiana companies to Mexico on four different trade missions. Later I worked 45 days in Florence, Italy, at the Commercial Service at the U.S. Consulate. I represented U.S. companies during a building and construction show, and worked diligently with my clients in northern Indiana territory.

The tumbleweed had at long last taken root and blossomed! As an International Trade Specialist, I designed and successfully implemented "tailored" comprehensive export development programs for companies within Indiana who were interested in targeting overseas markets. This meant that I was creating an "integrated" export program for my clients.

It was a classic "win-win" scenario. I was successful only when my client companies were successful, and they were successful when they exported more products to more countries than they had been doing without my help.

I presented regional export seminars, one-on-one counseling, and developed export assistance plans. I'd target export promotion events so I could prepare my clients and take them into key foreign markets.

This was a world the tumbleweed was uniquely qualified for. After all, I had lived my youth in Europe – on both sides of the Iron Curtain. I knew a language and culture outside of the American, and I could appreciate how foreign markets might react to American products. For the first time, in a professional work environment it was "who I am" that blended perfectly with what I was doing.

During those years, my programs resulted in Indiana companies generating export sales and establishing new distribution channels for their products and services. Daily I was interacting with our overseas colleagues at U.S. embassies all over the world and my work with the companies and other international trade partners in our state made it an exciting place to work. But I'm getting ahead of myself here. The tumbleweed had some other surprising changes on the horizon. My post-cancer life was just getting started.

In April 1994, after all my treatments were completed, we flew to California to visit our son Eric on his birthday. We had a wonderful time. While there we visited Robert Schuler's church one Sunday morning. I had been watching his "Hour of Power" show every week on TV at home during my treatments. That was – at the time -- the closest I could come to attending Church.

I hadn't given up on finding a place to worship the God I had gotten to know so much better while undergoing the treatments. I came across a wonderfully inspiring poem in those dark days. It's called "Footprints in the Sand." It talks about Jesus actually carrying you when times are toughest and you think you're alone. I felt like that poem was written just for me. I now have a *Footprints in the Sand* figurine in my curio cabinet. When I look at it, I'm reminded of those troubling days of my cancer and chemotherapy. But, as we returned from California where we had heard Robert Schuler preach about "Coming Home Again," more surprises were in store.

Before the trip Wes had kenneled our dog, Sascha, a few miles from our Indiana home. When we returned from California, he went to pick up our Cocker. As he came back with Sascha, he asked me, "Did you know that there is a new Catholic Church just behind the kennel?"

"No," I replied. I hadn't told Wes that I had been praying at night for him to return to Church. I held my breath.

"Would you like to go to Mass on a Sunday?" he asked.

I thought I hadn't heard him right. Wes wants to go to Mass? Did God really hear my prayers?

"Of course. Let's go on Sunday," I said.

The following Sunday we attended Mass at the new Church behind the kennel. The Church was located on a 28-acre lot, with an entrance driveway between two ponds and water fountains shooting water up into the air. As we approached the Church, the building looked as if there were two outstretched arms welcoming us. It was a breath-taking setting.

Inside, Wes couldn't believe what he saw at the Mass. The Catholic Church had changed so much since Vatican II, when he had rather firmly, and without looking back, closed the door behind him. He remembered the worship service in Latin and the priest facing an altar at the rear wall. Here, in this "new" Catholic Church, people were singing enthusiastically and in English. And the priest gave his homily while walking in front of the congregation.

And most shocking of all, "What are all those people doing up on the altar?" Wes whispered almost in shock.

I didn't know it at the time, but the people who had caught his eye were Eucharistic ministers. They were assisting the priest with the giving of communion. It was a beautiful morning.

"Would you like to try the Mass for 10 Sundays to see if we like it," Wes asked on the way home. He had been away from the Church for thirty years.

"I would love it," I replied, holding back my tears.

"Is it really that easy that God listens to prayers?" I asked myself.

I couldn't wait for next Sunday to come. We attended three Sunday Masses and liked it so well that we became members of that Church. The Priest played a key role in our decision. He is a Priest we will never forget.

In September 1994 I started classes and became a Catholic the following Easter. Wes was my sponsor and a "refresher student" at the same time. Six years later I was one of those Eucharistic Ministers, Wes was a lector, and I took on an Arts and Environment ministry. This ministry allowed me to use my artistic talents for the Church. I was using color, symbols, flowers, and decorations to help our faith community to fully experience the theme of the liturgy. For special Holy Days, Feast Days, and the Liturgical Seasons I spent hours upon hours putting up decorative floral arrangements, colored fabric, plants, trees, even burlap "hills" at Lent. Wes helped me with all of this as we became very active and involved members of our church.

This 10-year church ministry complemented my hobby that I have loved for years. I am an artist, painting in various media. I had started this hobby in 1978 while stationed at Ramstein Air Base. My career there kept me so busy that I could devote only a few hours here and there for my art. It is a hobby that I am now pursuing during my retirement years.

Back at work, and at age 51 in 2004, my goal and my dream came to fruition. I earned a promotion to Senior International Trade Specialist, GS-13. I had reached a professional career plateau, equivalent to a Master's Degree. Yes, it is true in this beautiful country. You can be whoever you dream to be. You can become whatever you want to become, if you are willing to work at it. I love the United States. There is no other country in the world that even comes close to the freedom and the opportunities we have, and the generosity it offers to the entire world. I often cry at football games or parades when thousands of people get together peacefully. I feel like kissing the ground whenever I return from trips outside the country. I am proud to be an American now. However, I will always be connected to Germany and won't forget my heritage.

Born and raised in Germany, I have all along been faced with the need to "re-educate" myself--starting with language. Since all of my schooling through high school was in my native German language, the transition to my present position was a difficult one. Unable at first to read or write with sufficient fluency for English-language secretarial jobs, I first took jobs in restaurants and "earned" while I "learned." Later, I took a course in cosmetology competing with American educated high school graduates and finished at the top of class for both academic and practical work. I was chosen as Miss Cosmetology. Finally, I began at the GS-3 level and worked my way to a position which requires a undergraduate/master's degrees. I struggled and worked harder than many other people. I survived the interference of those people who had envied me and who had tried to make me fail. I felt humiliated many times. I experienced the lack of communication skills which hindered me from defending myself verbally while absorbing assaults of people including my own mother-in-law who once called me a "stupid fish wife."

In my jobs I was often resented because I couldn't "play" while working. My culture has taught me that when you work, you work, and when you play you play.

I was accused of setting the standards too high for others though such was never my intention. Each time I fell, I got up and leaped over yet another hurdle. Yes, I am a survivor. A survivor at work, a survivor of cancer, and a survivor of cultural change.

I thank my courageous parents and the risks they took by fleeing East Germany with its communist domination. They left behind everything that my father, then 32, had spent his life working for and all the hopes and dreams my mother had once been so sure of.

I am the embodiment of the three cultures which have shaped my life: the former East Bloc "managed economy" of post-WWII East Germany, the "economic miracle" of West Germany's re-emergence into a market economy, and the robust free enterprise American system. I AM A TUMBLEWEED!!

---END---

Epilogue

In April 1989 –six months before the Berlin Wall "came down"—Wes' school was on spring break. We flew to Germany to celebrate our 25th wedding anniversary. We had only a week for our visit, but Wes insisted that we visit Berlin on at least one of those days. We wanted to try to re-trace the route of my family's escape.

As it turned out, we went "behind the wall" and for the first time since my escape I found myself enmeshed in fear and silence. The whispering like that in Mama's house in Kleinforst, the eyes that quickly looked away, and armed guards with grim faces, all of this made me feel trapped as I had not felt since the harrowing days of our escape.

I had never seen the "wall" as it existed after the 1961 "improvements." At the time I and my family escaped, Berlin was closely controlled with checkpoints like the one Mutti and I had slipped through, but the "concrete" walls following 1961 had made the border nearly impenetrable. Very few made it through.

The post-1961 Berlin Wall was a double-walled concrete barrier. With Russian oversight and assistance, it was built by German Democratic Republic (GDR) engineers guarded by what we called "Vopos." That was an informal term for Volkspolizei, or People's Police. The "modern" wall completely enclosed the free city of West Berlin, separating it from both the East German countryside and the city of East Berlin.

The wall was much more than most people imagined. And it was far more than a barrier around Berlin. It was, in fact, but one segment of the Iron Curtain with its 4,250 mile length extending from the Arctic to the Black Sea.

The Wall included guard towers spaced "machine-gun" distance from one another. Even outside Berlin, in places where population density posed a threat of escape, concrete walls circumscribed wide areas. Most westerners mistakenly called it "the" Berlin Wall, or "the" Iron Curtain, as if this gargantuan jail-like barrier was "singular." But it wasn't singular. It was double. It was almost entirely two walls separated by what later would be known as the "death" strip.

This strip contained anti-vehicle trenches, tank traps, land mines, electric fences, razor-sharp fence segments, and other defenses.

Many years after my refugee-camp experiences, I had seen the "iron curtain" (barbed wire) well beyond the better known Berlin wall. Wes and I traveled north beyond Hannover to Ohrdorf, in the northern German state of Niedersachsen (Lower Saxony) where my parents lived after they moved away from Hirschfeld.

On one of those trips Wes and I visited a border town called Zicherie. Locals called it "Little Berlin." This little town had been split in two by the border installations. There were large signs warning "Halt Zonengrenze." An imposing concrete watchtower had been erected in the middle of what had once been a street. That street was now the "death strip" dividing the village and it housed armed East German border guards.

These guards, along with other East Germans, had been brainwashed into believing that the iron curtain with all its barbed wire, watch towers and guards were there to prevent West Germans from fleeing in to their country. What an irony.

The record books do not contain a single case of anyone escaping east over this barrier. Who would want to flee into a country that was run by a Communist regime that kept its own people hostage?

So it was with some trepidation that Wes and I flew from Braunschweig to West Berlin that April week of 1989. He needed to find a place along the wall where someone – a fictional western agent -- could jump over the wall from the West to the East side of Berlin. This was for a Cold War spy novel he was writing.

We took several pictures of the wall near Potsdamer Platz near where Wes found the perfect place for his fictional scene. At the same time it gave us the opportunity to look for several places I hadn't seen since I and my family were at the refugee camp in 1955.

I saw the sharp contrast between the two worlds divided by the wall, and yes, we also saw the industrial building which had been my refugee camp. It had been returned to an electric products assembly plant.

On our way back to the Berlin airport, we decided to take the subway under East Berlin. On the map, this looked like a shortcut. Wes felt that since he no longer was in the military, he wasn't obligated to go through Check Point Charlie, and the map showed the subway line passing under East Berlin.

What the map did not show, however, was that we would have to disembark from one train, step into East Berlin, and walk both underground and at surface-level under the watchful eyes of armed guards. This we had to do when we arrived at Friedrichstrasse, the East German border station.

The subway station was gray and cold, not at all like the West Berlin subway station that had lots of color and stores for last-minute purchases. On the way to the above ground train track, we noticed a large door with a sign "Halt, Zonengrenze" which meant "Stop, Border." An East German border guard with a machine gun stood in front of the door. As I was trying to take his picture he yelled at me, "Fotografieren verboten (not allowed to take pictures)."

Cold chills ran down my body. I was afraid he would take us in and we would never be seen again. (In truth, he could have legally detained us for 48 hours.)

As we came upstairs to the main station, we noticed two tracks. One was for East Germans only and the other was for West Berliners or tourists who changed trains to get back into West Berlin.

Guard posts high up in each of the station's four corners housed guards hovering over mounted machine guns. Their job was to watch for and deter any East Germans who might attempt jumping the track and escaping to the West.

In the distance, through broken and coal-stained glass, we saw gray looking large block houses in desperate need of repair. It was a sign that East Germans didn't have money or supplies to fix the old buildings. To me it seemed that East Berlin had not changed over the past 40 years even though it had become the showcase for the German Democratic Republic.

I found myself remembering what my father many years earlier had said about the German Democratic Republic, that only the word "German" could be said to be true.

While we were waiting for the next train to take us out of East Berlin and away from Friedrichstrasse, armed guards passed us as they patrolled the station. Wes told me they were carrying the Polish version of the "Uzi" machine gun. Their uniform sleeves were embroidered with, "Grenztruppen der Deutsche Demokratische Republik." (Border troops of the GDR.)

We noticed one person – a civilian wearing a short-waisted black leather jacket. He didn't take his eyes off of us. He followed us as we walked up and down the track as we were trying to keep warm. April wasn't summer yet and the temperature was a little chilly.

Wes watched as the man bought a newspaper at the kiosk. As the fellow took his wallet out of his pocket, it was obvious that he had an American-size wallet. The German Marks didn't fit snugly in the bill compartment because German Marks were much larger than U.S. dollar bills.

We knew at that point that he was an American. No German would allow his blue-colored 100-Mark bills to show so indiscreetly. We decided he was very likely an American spy. That would not have been unusual, on either side of the wall in Berlin. He might have noticed us and wondered why two Americans were waiting on a train platform in East Berlin.

The train finally arrived after 45 minutes which to me seemed 45 hours. The man followed us onto the train. We don't know how far he rode the train since Wes and I stepped off at the first stop in West Berlin, Lehrter Bahnhof, just across the Spree River. (Interesting aside: the Lehrter Bahnhof is now the site of Berlin's main train station, the Hauptbahnhof, after many years of reconstruction following the wall's demise.)

Shaken from the whole ordeal with the guards, the guns, the silence of the East Berlin train platform, we entered into the first West Berlin pub we could find and had a glass of beer to calm ourselves from our chilling experience at the Friedrichstrasse station. For both of us, it clarified once again why my parents had chosen to flee.

Back in "the West" our 25th wedding anniversary was a beautiful event having my brothers and their families joined together with my parents after several years of separation brought about by my absence from Germany. The one week we had was just too short, but it was better than nothing.

I missed having my family close by, but America had become my home. When we returned to Indiana our kids surprised us with balloons and gifts. Iris had come from Missouri and Eric from Indiana's Rose Hulman University where he was a student. We had a wonderful weekend which made me forget my homesickness for Germany.

Three weeks after our return, however, we had another major surprise. As we were taking a look at our trip photos, we noticed something startling among the pictures we took from the Berlin wall near Checkpoint Charlie.

Among the graffiti painted on the wall's western side, there in orange spray paint, were both of our kids' names! We had not seen that when taking the picture. Their names were written in large letters mixed with several layers of all manner of graffiti. The name Iris is not that common in German nor was the name Eric spelled with a "c." Yet there they were!

I almost fainted when Wes showed me the photo. What were the odds of finding both of our kids' names in one photograph of a concrete barrier that was over 100 miles long?

Neither Iris nor Eric had, at that time, even been to Berlin. But on our 25th wedding anniversary we find their names painted on the concrete border, the very border from which I and my parents had escaped!

This just seemed to bring my life full-circle. I escaped to West Germany to experience freedom. Freedom the Berlin Wall was built to prevent. The hated border had brought me closer to Wes and enabled me to be thankful for all the opportunities I had been given. Without the separation between West and East Germany, our children would not have been born. And there were my children's names almost within arm's reach of the American crossing point, Checkpoint Charlie!

Who would have known that six months following our silver anniversary trip, on the 9th of November, 1989, the wall would begin to be chipped away?

On that memorable day, I was on the way home from work in Indianapolis when I heard on the radio that East Berliners were standing atop the Berlin wall. I turned the radio louder since I thought I had not heard right. My first emotions raved through my body. There was happiness and hope that the East Germans would be freed, but also anger that we had had to endure all the suffering and pain for so many years.

My tears were rushing down my cheeks. I couldn't wait to get home and call my parents, Wes and our kids to let them know what I had heard.

But at home, I couldn't seem to reach any of them to share my excitement. I turned on the TV and saw Tom Brokaw covering the story from Berlin. The dramatic opening of the Berlin Wall was broadcast to stunned audiences around the globe.

East Germans were pouring into West Berlin like water bursting through a dam. Young people were standing on the wall and attacking it with any tool they could find. There was a celebration between East and West Berlin unlike anything anyone had ever seen, and best of all, no blood was shed.

The East German government had announced, after several weeks of civil unrest, that visits in West Germany and West Berlin would be permitted.

Every East German who came across into the West was given DM100. All they had to do was show their passports and have them stamped! The stores couldn't keep up with the overflow of people. Food ran out in hot dog stands and restaurants.

The scenery looked like birds flying out of cages into the free space. It wasn't long before I read an article reporting, "The fall of the Berlin Wall paved the way for German reunification, which was formally concluded on October 3,

1990. These iconic moments changed the world and appeared to give a sense of closure to a brutal and chaotic century.

This vast, fortified border system had marked the physical boundary between two geopolitical systems that were locked in a Cold War for nearly half a century."

At the time the wall came down on that historic November 9, 1989, I had not seen any of my extended family for some 33 years, except for a rarely-permitted visit by two of my uncles. In an uncharacteristic moment of compassion, the communist regime permitted two uncles, without their wives or children, to come to the west for my grandmother's funeral. Their mother, that resourceful Kleinforst grandmother I called "Mama," had died after living many years in West Germany.

At the time of her death Wes was stationed at Ramstein when my uncle Al, my mother's brother, came and visited us. Wes had contacted the OSI on base because he was required to let them know of our visitor from East Germany. Wes had asked if we could take him to the Officer's Club for dinner. They didn't have any objection.

We entered the main gate on base where we pointed to several large C-5 Galaxy aircraft that were parked on the flight line. Uncle Al however, didn't even turn his head. He looked straight ahead like a frozen puppet. He didn't want to know anything that he would have to divulge during the interrogation he knew would follow once he returned home in the communist East.

The conversation in the Club restaurant consisted mostly of reminiscing. We spoke of his childhood and mine. Al was five years older than I, and I remembered several activities with him at my grandmother's house in Kleinforst. He didn't speak too much but mainly listened to me.

As we ate, we noticed a man in a suit sitting behind Uncle Al. Both that man and Uncle Al were eating spaghetti. The man was leaning backwards in such a way that his spaghetti fell off his fork and onto his shirt and tie! It was so obvious that he was trying to listen to our conversation. We pegged him as an OSI agent since they had known that we were going to the Club. He must have been new at the spy business.

Al stayed a couple of days with us. He talked about his Dacha that he built for himself from scratch material obtained by bartering. His Dacha (an elaborate garden shed from the outside, but comfy cabin inside) was his refuge during the summer months. There he could be alone, away from the stressful East German living conditions. We took him on a trip to Trier and since Luxembourg was close by, we decided to take him there as well, only to find out that he, as a GDR citizen, was not allowed to enter that country without a proper visa. It signaled to him that he was not welcome in the Western world and he became even more silent.

As a farewell present, Wes bought him a Black and Decker drill set, a bottle of Whiskey, and a tape with music for his teenage daughter. At first he was hesitant in taking the items. He was afraid that they might get confiscated at the border. But then he took them anyway. We learned later that he bartered the bottle of whiskey for some bricks for his Dacha. The next time we would see Uncle Al would be many years later, after the fall of the Iron Curtain.

That opportunity arrived in June, 1991, after the reunification of the two Germanys so long separated by the iron curtain. Wes and I made another trip to Germany. At that time our son-in-law Lewis was stationed in Germany at Ramstein Air Base after he had served four years as Missile Officer in Missouri. He had cross-trained into the Intelligence field and soon found himself stationed in Germany.

So, our daughter Iris was living just a few miles from her own place of birth near Hirschfeld. Our son Eric had graduated from Rose Hulman and was working as an Electrical Engineer in the Los Angeles area. We planned for Eric to join us so we could all meet at Iris'. I wanted to show my children where I was born since the border was now open. There were a number of surprises on that trip, but the one least anticipated had nothing to do with the former iron curtain.

Eric brought a surprise from California -- his girlfriend – who joined him on his trip to Germany. He had just recently met her on a blind date. We had the good fortune to meet the young lady for the first time at the Frankfurt airport.

It was a very hot summer. No air conditioning in the car or in the house. A rare German heat wave made conditions a bit unbearable, but we all stuffed it out. Chele, his girlfriend, was a good trooper and hung in there visiting our family while being introduced to the German tempers, flaring a bit in the unusual blast of summer heat.

We all met at Iris' home in the hill country of Rheinland Pfalz, and from there we took the trip to Kleinforst, my birthplace. I hadn't seen my village for over 35 years. We crossed the former "border" at Helmstedt, the old checkpoint from West to East, and marveled at the simplicity of entering what for so many years had been the forbidden land.

Wes described our journey this way in an article for an Indiana newspaper:

"The autobahn adroitly swings to the left. Still visible are tall, slender, but now rusting light poles. They stand like silent sentries, ghosts of the Warsaw Pact. We see a vacant watchtower. Now it looks like a press box at an abandoned football field. Gone are the guards, the guns, and all the menacing features of the Iron Curtain.

"Is that the border? That is it?" I asked astonished to see how little remained of the more than 800+ mile system of guard towers and weapons which had cut me off from my home. In less than a minute at 60 m.p.h. we had entered one of Germany's five new states; Sachsen-Anhalt. We had to cross Sachsen-Anhalt to reach my hometown in Sachsen (Saxony).

Long before reaching the state of Sachsen, we began to form impressions of what "the new Germany" is like. We had already learned from friends and relatives in the "west" that all is not sugar-and-cream in this new cup of German coffee.

"The NBL, that's what we call the five new states," my brother told us. He pronounced it "en-bay-el." We heard the acronym often during our three-week stay. It's short for "Neue Bundes Laender," or New Federal States. Alone, it expresses little of an attitude, but "NBL" always seems to be accompanied by "they," or "them, over there." We did not hear the word "we" in discussions about "them, over there."

So, when we crossed into the former "East Germany," we found ourselves looking for differences. And we discovered "differences"—affecting both sides of the former border—physical conditions, economic fears, and lack of trust. Before we reached our first rest stop, we were convinced that Germans will be working on this "economic miracle" for a long time to come.

First impressions are important, especially to the Sachsens (Saxons, Germans of that state) with whom we travelled. But they can be misleading. What we saw as we departed the Autobahn (interstate highway) was 45 years of faded color, dusty looking drab brown and grey houses and shops. We drove through villages with names like Stegelitz, Zeppernick, Loburg, and Lindau. Narrow winding streets challenged even our small Volkswagen. Cobblestone pavement rattled its rhythm under our tires.

"It feels like we're stepping back into history. An earlier Germany," I said. "They've done nothing to improve their homes, their towns," I continued. There it was again. That word "they."

"We couldn't. There were no building materials," Alfred, our Oschatz host later explained. "We couldn't buy paint, plaster, wood, new curtains, modern windows."

We began to learn the realities of life in socialism's "planned economy."

Alfred explained. "Our factories were producing materials and weapons for Cuba, for Communist-supported countries in Africa. Our industry was supporting the world socialist movement. Even the best of our agriculture, pork and grains, was exported. That's why our stores were often empty."

So what we saw as we approached towns like Zerbst and Wittenberg appeared generally unkempt. Not dirty. Not litter strewn. Just lacking maintenance and renovation. Weeds and tall grass grew around businesses and public buildings. An aged windowless Church in Zerbst was in ruins, weeds growing atop broken gothic walls.

In even greater state of disrepair was a chemical factory we saw on the outskirts of Wittenberg (the Martin Luther city). Fallen plaster, broken windows, smoke-blackened walls, rows of rusting pipes. "Dilapidated" was the only word to describe its condition. Even to the untrained eye, this plant was out of step with today's industrial standards.

"It can only be razed, completely dismantled, and built anew if it is to compete in the world market," I said.

"The same can be said of almost all the of the NBL's industry," added my father, expressing an often heard western opinion. And again, we had struck an exposed nerve. For later, Esther, my uncle's wife, offered a view shared by many on the east.

"That's the problem," she said. "The west wants wholesale replacement of everything here. Everything, from industry, to business practices, to methods of operation. They make us feel as if nothing we have is of value. The east wants to blend the best of both systems, but the west is forcing its standards on us"

We had seen evidence of Esther's "wholesale replacement" on the way to Oschatz. We stopped for lunch at Coswig, along the Elbe River. A sign over the door of a local

Gasthaus advertised Wesenthal, a west German beer from the Rhein River area.

"Everything is new in here," I noted. "The curtains, the tablecloths, the wood paneling."

We discovered later that west German brewers in order to expand distribution of their product, contract with the east German restaurants and offer complete renovation (much needed) right down to the printing of menus and training the staff, in exchange for exclusive rights to distribute their beer.

There was nothing in the gasthaus that couldn't be seen in any similar establishment in the west. It was like eating at McDonalds in another state. Many west German brewers—including world-renowned Bitburger Pils—are doing the same throughout the new states.

We saw more impact of investment from the west before we reached Sachsen. A few new factories and businesses have sprouted since last October's reunification, especially near the former border around cities like Magdeburg. And everywhere freshly painted, newly mounted signs announcing, "GmbH,"—the German equivalent of the British "Ltd"—proclaim the presence of capitalism in the NBL.

Physical conditions—the appearance of dwellings, shops, businesses, even churches and historic buildings—are improving. Construction is underway everywhere. Scaffolding surrounds the Albrecht Cathedral overlooking Meissen, the

Church of the Cross in Dresden, and numerous other monuments of Germany's past.

In each of the 20 towns and villages we passed through—we had taken the scenic "country" route—on the way to Oschatz, one or two freshly plastered houses caught our attention. "New windows, new curtains, fresh paint," I commented. "They're starting."

In Oschatz itself perhaps 10% to 15% of the homes have received a facelift in the past year.

"Of course," I smiled with obvious pride in the homeland I had not seen in 35 years. "These are Sachsens. They always were a step ahead of the rest of Germany."

What we had seen on the road to Oschatz convinced me that socialism kills individual initiative, takes the efforts of all in society, but gives little in return. Pride is the victim.

It was in Oschatz with Uncle Al and his wife Esther that we began to sense the economic fears of the people in the new states. Factories closing, unemployment, no market for east German goods, higher prices, lower wages and pensions, uncertainty about the future—such were the concerns of the people we met in the region between Leipzig and Dresden.

A couple in their mid-50s—they'd be called empty nesters in America—Al and Esther lived in a cramped three-room (not counting a galley kitchen and narrow bathroom) apartment. Fresh wallpaper, bright paint, new sofas, and their own very warm welcome greeted us.

Al was at the time of our visit, still employed. Yet millions of his fellow NBL Germans were already tasting the bitter fruit of capitalism—unemployment.

"Our factories are closing," Al lamented. "When the west exchanged the new Deutsche Mark for our east Marks, it had a stronger negative effect than what was expected. We in the east lost our customers. Nobody (Poland, Czechoslovakia, Romania, Russia) could buy our products. They can't pay in western currency."

"And the west doesn't want our products, we can't compete," he added.

I learned it isn't simply a question of the quality of goods produced. In part, there is the complication of standards and agreements being finalized among the European Community members. Too, there is this basic difference—in the socialist economy wares were produced without regard for profit. The issue was quotas, not cost effectiveness. In the capitalist west, the technology of marketing focuses on minimizing production costs to maximize profit.

"Sure," said Uncle Al. "We've a lot to learn about capitalism, but it isn't just that. At first the west would not accept even our agricultural products."

He told us that West Germany kept foodstuffs, especially dairy products, off the market in the west claiming quality was lacking, standards were lower.

"And now they want our products because they have discovered our products are more natural, 'bio-freundlich' (biologically friendly, or natural)," he smiled.

Agriculture was the one part of the economy that looked really healthy as we drove across the states Sachsen-Anhalt and Sachsen.   Fields of wheat, barley, and rye looked robust. Virtually every available field was planted with grain, healthy green in color, thick and fully developed. I decided to ask Al whether farming is now a private-enterprise venture.

"It is," he said. "Most of the former co-ops have become privately-owned enterprises. They're still co-ops, sharing heavy equipment, labor, and costs. They couldn't survive otherwise. Who could afford such large equipment?"

I told him my in-expert eye assessed this year's crop as healthy and robust. "Perhaps farming will be the first to turn a really stable profit," I ventured.

"Perhaps," he said. "If they can find a market for their goods."

Later, our conversation turned more personal. "What do you have in your stores now which was not available before 'the change'," I asked.

(Germans on both sides of the former border refer to "Die Wende,"—"the change"—rather than the more complex term for reunification, "Wiedervereinigung.")

"Everything!" Uncle Al exploded. "And no lines anymore!"

I had seen many obviously new "western" goods in the stores and on the streets—Japanese electronics, West German kitchen appliances, American compact-discs and cassette tapes, and, of course, Jeans. The smoky little Trabbis (compact cars) are disappearing (production has ceased), and new VW Golfs, BMWs, and even a few Hondas are appearing on East German streets.

"And how are prices now?" I asked.

Al's response was intense, animated. "Higher! For almost everything. Things we need every day—bread, gasoline, beer, all food—cost more now than before. Big items, the things you buy seldom, like refrigerators and washing machines are priced lower now. But, how often do you need a refrigerator?"

Al also said the locals "pay more for everything than they do in the west," voicing a commonly held East German opinion. "Prices are higher, and we earn less than comparable workers in the west."

Prices are certainly higher than they had been when subsidized under the communist economy. But I had noted prices for food, especially in restaurants, and for clothing, were 20% to 25% lower in the east than what I saw in the west.

Both Al and his wife, Esther, expressed doubts that the "Easties" were being treated fairly with respect to wages, and pension plans.

"Income here is far lower than it would be for the same work in the west. And our pensions will be based on actual income. We'll receive less than 'they' in the west will," both commented.

Economic woes—especially taxes—also worry the "westies," however. The financial impact of freedom for their eastern countrymen has tempered the initial euphoria of the wall coming down.

"My salary has been capped," a west teacher told us. "Since last year there has been a lid on all civil service income. And now our taxes are going up!"

Indeed, during our visit the newspapers reported a July 1 income tax increase of 7.5% while gasoline taxes went up 25-pfennig per liter—equating to a surge of 55 cents per gallon! Other government-provided services such as postage and telephone fees also increased. In January the sales tax is to climb from 14% to 16% (value added tax).

Now this "bottom line" contributes to a west attitude we heard expressed this way: "Their system failed. Now the easties want to benefit from our labor. We rebuilt Germany. We sweat and saved. Now our taxes, our savings, are being handed to them!"

This view ignores, of course, history. The "easties" did not choose their system—it was imposed upon them and enforced with guns and tanks.

We met only one man, an elderly emigrant from Poland who had spent most of his adult life running a small restaurant in Niedersachsen (West German), who clearly remembered the past.

"Of course!" his fist banged the tabletop. "Why can't we remember? They had no choice. The Russians made the decisions after the war. And Hitler before that! Why, those people haven't had any freedom since the Weimar Republic, before Hitler. And that didn't last very long!"

"Thank you, Her Ruge," I said. "I was beginning to think all this worry over taxes and costs had made everyone forget the "why" of it all."

Underlying all the concern over things economic and contributing to a lack of trust on the part of the "easties" is the presence—still—of Russian troops. We saw them daily in the east.

Only "66,000 of the 380,000 Russian troops have departed as of June," reported the Aller Zeitung, a western newspaper in its July 4 issue. The same day's Bild Zeitung, a national daily, reported, "...despite delays, the Soviet troops will be pulled out on time, according to Colonel Strelnikow, vice commander of Soviet West troops." The Soviet colonel explained "There is a shortage of apartments for the homeward bound troops."

We didn't need the newspaper reports, however, except perhaps for the numbers. Each day in the east we saw Soviet military convoys, troops, and aircraft.

At Zerbst, near Wittenberg, we saw a Russian airfield with a squadron of Mig-29s parked on the ramp (some 20 fighters quite similar in appearance to the USAF F-15). Next to them was in Ilyushin 76, the Soviet counterpart to the American C-141, a large transport jet.

Uncle Al was silent about the Russians, except to acknowledge in response to my question that, "Yes, some have departed. The air field at Oschatz is closed."

And indeed it was. We saw it the next day, vacated and looking as dilapidated as an Arizona ghost town.

"But they still have an option close by," I told Al, for I had seen a remarkably new section of the Autobahn between Dresden and Leipzig. The center median, level for nearly three miles, had been filled with concrete and was devoid of any obstruction that could hinder an airplane. "That piece of Autobahn could easily be used as a runway."

"Oh. You discovered that did you?" he smiled, a twinkle in his eyes. It was the only comment he made about the Russians. He saw them too. But he was silent.

"They've learned to be silent, and it's no wonder they lack trust," I later reminded Bübchen, my youngest brother. "They haven't forgotten 1953 in Berlin, 1956 in Hungary, 1968 in Czechoslovakia. It was Russian tanks, Russian troops which taught them to be silent."

"How would you feel," I asked Bübchen, "if the first thing you saw every morning on your way to work was Russian soldier?"

We had seen—in just a few days in the east—a 20-truck military convoy on the road between Oschatz and Meissen, numerous trucks and "jeeps" near Wittenberg, two Russian officers escorting three civilians at Morizburg Palace near Dresden, two low-flying Russian fighters over Meissen at noon, and a Russian work detail loading coal into trucks at the railway station in Oschatz. All that—aside from the airbase at Zerbst—without looking for them.

The "easties" see them every day—and we noticed they seem, almost intensely, not to see them. What they didn't want to see revealed the uneasiness. We felt more than heard the lack of trust.

With 314,000 Russian troops still there, with the deep disappointment in their now defunct communist leaders of the recent past, with the anger and disillusionment over the revelations of how the "Stasi" (state secret police) had assembled "secret files" on them, with uncertainty about their jobs, their wages, their pensions, with doubts about how free enterprise will benefit them, who can blame the people of the "NBL" if they lack trust even for their "westie" countrymen?

Like a good German wine, it will take years of careful tending to the vines, just the right blend of soil and moisture and sun, and the patience only a vintner knows, before "die Wende"—the change—produces the new Deutschland.

Today, at the time I am ready to publish "Tumbleweed," more than 20 years after Die Wende, the wine has fermented and is ready. A new Deutschland is emerged, stronger than ever. It took a lot of patience of both sides and it certainly was a miracle for the world to watch that this all happened without any bloodshed.

The tumbleweed's trip to "East Germany" was a trip to remember. My kids saw my birth place and were in awe at what they had seen. We returned to Iris' place in Soetern where we stayed another week. Eric and Chele took off on a train trip to France. They wanted to see Paris for a short sightseeing trip, and they returned with a big surprise.

With tears in his eyes Eric said in a squirrely voice, "I have to tell you something."

We all waited.

"I've proposed to Chele on the Eifel tower, and she has agreed to marry me."

"You just met her couple of months ago," I said. "Are you sure?"

I immediately realized what I had said. I had only known Wes three months in 1963 when he proposed to me, and I am sure my mother felt then just as I now did.

"I have to get a bottle of Champagne," Wes said and disappeared into the dark. When he returned he had one bottle in his hands.

"You wouldn't believe this. They had only one bottle in the Gasthaus, and this one is from Russia," he laughed. "It didn't take them very long to export their goods out," he continued.

With Russian Champagne, we toasted to the engagement and laughed and cried all at the same time. We didn't have crystal glasses to throw against the wall, as my mother had done when Wes and I got engaged. It didn't matter.

The next morning we all went on a ring-shopping trip to nearby Idar Oberstein, the gem capital of Germany.

So the tumbleweed returned to Kleinforst, my daughter was living practically next door to where she had been born, and my son celebrated his engagement on German soil.

What a journey it has all been!

Acknowledgements

I began writing this book early in the 80's when I gave interviews about my childhood years to military journalism students who were writing human interest feature stories. Many of these budding journalists at the Defense Information School encouraged me to write a book some day. My own career advancement and raising my family put the project on the back burner for several years.

Now the time has come to pass my story on to my children and grandchildren who deserve to know their heritage. I want to show them the challenges refugees and immigrants encounter no matter where they live, and teach them how to beat the odds when faced with a struggle for survival.

"Tumbleweed" records events I experienced as a young girl in Germany living first under the Communist regime, then within the "economic miracle" of West Germany, and finally my years as an immigrant and military spouse in the United States.

This is my story about people who live under extreme circumstances, people who conquer the fear of taking risks. The story is about being a refugee from East Germany trying to fit in and be accepted by fellow Germans on the other side of the iron curtain. The story is about an immigrant who despite a lack of English language skills learns the language then competes in the workplace and overcomes obstacles to career advancement in the world's most wonderful country. The story is about a young woman who encounters a life threatening disease and how she became a survivor.

I have a vivid memory of everything that has happened in my life. Maybe this is because I am an artist. Once I started to write, my memory was as if I would live it all over again.

While it is not possible to recount with exactitude specific words that were spoken in long-ago scenarios, the essential nature of each conversation has easily returned to memory making recalled commentary truthful even where perhaps not reproduced with "digital audio" accuracy. My mother, the "Mutti" of this story, has helped me to fill in those gaps where events of my youth preceded my ability to recall them in detail.

I thank God for his love and for having guided me throughout my life and who has never failed me. I thank my parents who have suffered and sacrificed so much in order for us to be free. I thank Wes, my husband and best friend, who supported me in writing this book and who has taught me so much. I thank my children and grandchildren who have brought me so much happiness and love. I thank my physicians who made the right diagnoses and recommended the right treatments. And finally I would like to thank the United States of America for being the greatest and most generous country in the world providing me the opportunities to become whatever I wanted to become and I what I have become.

Josefine Tilton

Credits: Some statistical data and some historical remarks related to the Cold War and to the Berlin Wall are to be credited to Wikipedia.com and to selected German newspapers we read during our travels to the "NBL." In most cases, our own memories (my mother, my husband, and my own) were sufficient but needed to be checked or verified with Wikipedia.com

About the Author

Now retired, Josefine Tilton was a Senior International Trade Specialist for the U.S. Department of Commerce office in Indianapolis, Indiana. There she culminated a distinguished 30-year career with the Federal Government. She was born, raised and educated in Germany. Mrs. Tilton attended the University of Maryland before holding Commerce Department positions. She had earlier graduated from the Traben-Trarbach School of Commerce in the State of Rheinland-Pfalz, Germany. She is the embodiment of the three cultures which have shaped her life -- the former East Bloc "managed economy" of post WWII (escaped East Germany in 1955), the "economic miracle" of West Germany's re-emergence into a market economy, and the robust free enterprise American system. She joined the United States Department of Commerce, and became an icon of success within the International Trade Administration/U.S. & Foreign Commercial Service. As an International Trade Specialist, Mrs. Tilton crafted comprehensive export development programs for Indiana companies seeking overseas markets. She did this to introduce her clients into key foreign markets. Her success was measured by her many clients who gained export sales and established new distribution channels for their products. Earlier in her Federal Government career she had assignments for the Department of Defense. These were at U.S. Air Forces Headquarters in Europe and at the Defense Information School at Fort Benjamin Harrison in Indianapolis. She is married, has two children and four grandchildren. She is an artist of various media and currently is represented in several galleries within Virginia particularly in the northern Shenandoah Valley.

Made in the USA
Middletown, DE
01 November 2023

41649990R00168